Holding the Fort Abroad

Beyond Surviving – living and parenting abroad with a partner who works away from home

Rhoda Bangerter

First published in Great Britain by Summertime Publishing

ISBN: 978-1-8381670-1-1

Cover and internal pages designed by Cath Brew at drawntoastory.com

*To Olivier
and the two precious boys in our life.*

Acknowledgements

There are so many people I would like to thank.

To Colleen Higgs, Ute Limacher-Riebold, Sundae Schneider-Bean, Andrea Schmitt, Carolyn Parse Rizzo, Vici Tanner, Mariam Ottimofiore, Helen Ellis, Annabelle Humanes, Caron, Regina, Cindy, Luke, Nicolena, Renera, Noelle, Valentina, and all those who answered the 'Holding the Fort Abroad Survey': thank you for giving of your time and sharing your life journeys. To Béatrice de Carpentier for your input as Marriage Counsellor and Dawn Purver as Psychotherapist.

Amel Derragui, you are fantastic! When I first reached out, I wasn't 100% committed to a vision. One conversation with you led me to clearly know the community I wanted to serve. I haven't looked back.

Jo Parfitt, thank you for encouraging me to go ahead with this endeavour, for your rigorous editing and for everything I have learned in your wonderful Writing Circle. I'm grateful for the friendships formed in that group.

Cath Brew, thank you for the wonderful book cover. My husband and I love it. It pulls on the heartstrings. Someone is clearly absent yet their presence is felt. It also shows different realities lived in different time zones and locations, yet lives are joined together under one roof. We feel it captures the essence of living as a family with a travelling partner.

To my therapist, thank you from the bottom of my heart for accompanying me through the juggling act/roller coaster that has been my life these past years. The things I have learned through our sessions have helped me through difficult times and shown me a path to growth.

To Hannah, thank you for sticking with me, for all your excellent work as a Virtual Assistant, for laughs and too many voice messages to count. I'll never forget how funny it was the time you found an officiating official and the word 'spouse' used seven times in a single paragraph!

Myriam, who would have thought our friendship through various continents would lead us here. Not only have you encouraged me to write this book from the get-go, you helped at a pivotal moment with your exceptional eye for content editing. Thank you.

To Mark, Susan and Hamish (aka 'The Hamishes'), Bob and Lilo, Mo, Richard and Elisabeth, love being family abroad with you guys.

Julie, in nearly twenty years of friendship, you've become a sister. We know each other pretty well, I'd say. Thank you for all the conversations and being my sounding board. Your and Q's prayers are precious.

Acknowledgements

To Dad, for giving me the love of books and writing. I miss our long conversations. See you in heaven. Mum, you did great raising three children abroad. We are okay.

Matt and Lydia, living in three different countries can't separate siblings who love each other. Thanks for the WhatsApp chats and for always having my back.

Margrit and Willy, you are the best parents-in-law. Thank you for welcoming me into your family with open arms.

To the Strength greater than my own. I often wander off but when I lean in, you are there. You helped me through the darkest moments.

Olivier, without you, this wouldn't have been possible. Literally because of all the travel you do, you provided the topic. Seriously, thank you for backing my dream, believing in me and supporting it with practical help. We make a great team. I love you.

To you, Olivier, and the two precious boys in our life, this book is dedicated to you.

Contents

Foreword

Through my practice I support many men and women with partners who are away for long periods of time and notice the situation is on the increase. This can be stressful; partners may have negative self-talk and experience a variety of difficult emotions. I help them to reframe their story and see that, in truth, their role is one of healing and the part they play, their input, their effort in the family dynamic, is critical to its success. *Holding the Fort Abroad* empowers the partner and recognises the significance and importance of the role. Now, thanks to this book, their voices can be heard.

Rhoda has lived and continues to live this life. As she was writing her family went through trauma, loss, fear and ill-health, and yet she did not write simply from her experience. She conducted interviews, ran a survey and reached out to others in her position. Further, she added expertise from well-respected colleagues in the field of intercultural transition, coaching, parenting and psychology to the 'art of her heart'. Immediacy and truth combine with science – the perfect combination.

This book is about far more than solo-parenting. It's about ageing parents, identity, romance and continuing to feel like a partnership. *Holding the Fort Abroad* is a comprehensive guide to developing resilience and is filled with information, advice and practical tips. It is empowering, encouraging and easy to read.

The main message here is that your partner may be absent but love is never gone. Yes, it changes because of time and distance, but it does not leave you. Love knows no borders. Rhoda's message needs to be heard.

Vivian Chiona
Director and Founder of Expat Nest www.expatnest.com

Who This Book Is For

Holding the Fort Abroad is mainly written with the 'at home' expat parent in mind. Whether they have a paid job or not, they are the constant parent if their partner travels in and out of the home. Being away from extended family, living cross-culturally and friendships constantly shifting because of moves means that absences due to work travel feel different. Though it is not written from their perspective, the travelling partner will gain insight on what goes on when they are away and pick up ideas on how to remain engaged with the family (see *The Travelling Parent, Chapter 5*). Some of the challenges will seem familiar for couples not living abroad yet who are also frequently apart.

The final chapter of this book is for families who have decided to live in split locations. Although my husband has travelled different amounts at various times, this is what we are living now. I call it 'The Marathon' because separations are for six weeks or more, over an extended period of time. During the writing of this book, the coronavirus has ripped through the world and many couples have found themselves geographically separated. A lot of the practical advice in the book applies to them as well.

In *Two Travellers* (*Chapter 3*), I have broached the subject of couples who both travel for work. There are couples living abroad who are successfully doing this. If this is what you aspire to but don't know where to start, *Keep Growing* (*Chapter 2*) will help and *A Successful Portable Business* (*Chapter 2*) takes it a little further and could present a solution by becoming a dual-career couple.

Couples where one partner works long hours will also enjoy reading this book as some of the challenges will resonate with them, particularly topics like feeling like a family, staying strong as a couple (*Chapter 3: One Couple*) and the overwhelm for the parent shouldering most of the responsibilities for the children (*The Constant Parent*, *Chapter 5*).

Intercultural families will find information about hidden sources of tension (*Chapter 3: One Couple*). And sometimes, as having a partner away on a trip does not exempt anyone from extra-trying times like illness abroad, losing a loved one, taking care of ageing parents or dangerous locations, those situations are covered as well (*Chapter 4: When Storms Come*).

If you know anyone with a travelling partner, this book may help you understand some of their reality. And if you don't (yet), you might just discover them as you talk to friends and family about reading this book!

And as one of the members of the 'Solo Parenting Expat Mums' Facebook group put it: "some of the information is useful for any couple!"

Introduction

Holding the fort, or, in American English, *holding down the fort*, is an expression that means taking care of things during someone's absence.

In March 2019, as my husband prepared to live in Afghanistan for two years while I stayed in Switzerland, I realised that he has travelled for work throughout our 15-year marriage, albeit not eight weeks at a time, as we were then planning. It would be fair to say I took care of home, family and my own projects while he was away.

There have been times when I arrived with our two boys at the location of my husband's new posting and he was already off on a work trip. In the meantime, I found a home, transitioned the children into a new school and settled in. Or the other way around: he went on to his new job while I sold the house, organised the goodbyes and shipped us all off to our new destination.

Over the years, I have had conversations with fellow globally mobile families about the fact that often, a big part of a posting includes work travel. Frequent business travel is mentioned, along with loss of social network, loneliness and resentment as typical stresses of expatriation on the Accompanying Partner. But its impact is rarely looked at separately. It is high time we start talking, in its own right, about life abroad with a travelling partner.

> It is high time we start talking,
> in its own right, about life abroad
> with a travelling partner.

For some expats, their assignment location might actually signal the end of work travel but there may nevertheless be stints of solo parenting as one parent returns to the 'home' country for the summer vacation or a few months before the end of an overseas posting.

The challenge, whether our partners are gone a few days or many weeks, is to maintain connection as a couple, to parent together, even at a distance, and not get overwhelmed with 24/7 parenting. Living abroad, with languages we are learning and for many, as an intercultural couple, adds layers of challenges for many globally mobile families.

This book is not meant to be exhaustive, describing every practical tip useful for the solo parent abroad. Nor is it a thorough examination of every possible scenario.

What you have in your hands is a decade and a half's worth of personal experience. Interwoven in each chapter you'll find stories of people living like us and who share insights, highlight struggles and point to solutions that have helped. Some answers from my ongoing survey, 'The Holding the Fort Abroad Survey', have also been included. Some names have been changed for privacy.

Introduction

I have delved into as much academic research on the subject as I could find and have drawn from books and articles on single parenting, long-distance relationships, military families, co-parenting resources for divorced couples who do not live close to each other and books for families where one or both parents travel frequently for work.

May you be inspired and encouraged.

Know, above all, that you are not alone. Many walk this path. If you are in 'survival mode', just wanting to get through the day, there is a tribe out there that understands.

Chapter 1
A Suitcase by the Door

"Maybe it's a good idea to write something about you in my book. At least then there will be a place where we will meet every day and be together forever!"
ANAMIKA MISHRA

Bern, Switzerland, 2013
"Knock, Knock," I hear from my position at the kitchen sink, then a handle being rattled as someone tries to open the front door of our apartment.

My heart skips a beat. It can only be one person: Olivier is due back today. He must be at the door.

I turn the key in the lock and fling the door of our home and of my heart wide open. Standing there, with a smile on his face, is my green-eyed, 6'3", rugged husband. He throws his arms around me and I bury my face in his neck, breathing in the familiar and comforting smell of his aftershave.

He walks in, wheeling his heavy suitcase and lays it in the middle of the hallway, along with an array of plastic bags, his carry-on and his jacket. Our eyes meet above the mess and we smile as both boys bounce all around us, desperate to 'tell Papa something'.

1

"Welcome home," I manage, over the noise.

He will be unpacking in a few minutes and the contents of his bags will be strewn across our hallway floor as the boys and I hover around peppering him with questions.

"These treats are for the office," he says, laying down boxes of baklava in a pile. Then, "This is for us, as a family."

Yummy, I think. I love tasting foods from the places he has been to.

We continue sorting: clothes in the washroom, notebooks, and papers set aside to be organised.

Within 20 minutes, his suitcase is empty, ready for his next departure.

The Revolving Door

When we were first married, Olivier worked for a humanitarian organisation. He travelled one to two weeks every few months, often to conflict areas. The twist was that he was on emergency call; he could leave within 24 hours to a country in crisis, either because a war had just broken out or a natural disaster had occurred. We had both agreed that he would join that particular list, so that didn't come as a surprise.

A few years later, after our second son was born, Olivier got a job in Bern, about an hour and a half's drive away.

A Suitcase by the Door

He went ahead and I stayed with our boys to organise the viewings of the home we were selling. He travelled back and forth, Monday to Friday, every week. This type of travel has a specific set of challenges as the commuter transitions in and out at weekends. Two days (two and a half days tops) doesn't give anyone much time to reconnect. Time as a couple is reduced to close to zero and exhaustion sets in from the commute at the beginning and end of every week. The financial pressure of selling and buying a home adds to the stress. The advantages though, are that most of the people around you can understand this kind of travel. It is regular and predictable, so extra help with babysitting or household chores can be arranged, if needed, on a regular basis.

Our children got so used to the rhythm that when we eventually did move, our eldest son nearly jumped out of his skin when his dad walked in on a Monday evening.

"You're not supposed to be here!" our five-year-old cried out, bewildered.

"This is the new normal," I explained to him. "Isn't it great?"

We thought our little one had understood that Papa would be coming home every evening but he was obviously not quite prepared for the reality of it.

Eighteen months after moving to Bern, we were packing our bags and moving to New York as Olivier was going

3

to work for the United Nations. Soon after we landed, he was already jetting off by plane for a work-related trip and I figured out how to go from East 81st Street to East 23rd Street with a stroller and two children (a two-year-old and a five-year-old). I had three weeks to find a new school and a new home before the shipped container with our belongings arrived.

During our two and a half years in New York, Olivier travelled to almost every continent. Although I was living in an iconic city (and made the most of what it had to offer), these were the years that I was most jealous of his travels. Seeing a photo of him eating sushi in Japan got my juices flowing with envy.

In 2016, back in Europe, he started travelling irregularly, two or three days a week. You would think this was easier and that he was travelling less. For me though, it meant that every week was different. It was a bit of a nightmare because even with carefully laid out plans and great communication between us as we pored over our diaries, work demands would change, and we'd be left scrambling to reorganise.

Unpredictable frequency, by far, is my least favourite work-travel setup. It's funny, because Olivier doesn't remember travelling much at all that year. For him, it was the least amount of travel he has ever done. To all intents and purposes, he felt he was genuinely 'living at home'.

2019 to 2021 is another story. We live in two separate countries and he comes home every eight to ten weeks for one or two weeks. Totally different ballgame. In some way, I prefer being apart longer rather than shorter. Even though it feels more like a marathon there is no doubt that it is easier to plan. Again, I'm surprised at how common my situation is. It is just not talked about much. You may hear it mentioned in conversation, and usually in the past tense.

"Oh, yes, when my husband was living in America and I was in France with the kids," someone would say.

Wait, what? I would think. *This person is saying it like it was no big deal.*

If I wasn't living it, I might have completely missed it in the conversation. Some couples may not think it's worth mentioning and if you are just an acquaintance, you may never know that the mum you chit-chat with every morning at school is actually solo parenting most of the time.

"12% of expats in a relationship are not living in the same country as their partner," reports 'Expat Insider 2018', one of the world's largest and most comprehensive surveys of life abroad. This percentage is set to increase because families considering expatriation are concerned about the Accompanying Partner's career and the safety and security of the new location. Families may decide to split locations to ensure ease of access to medical facilities if needed or to 'safer' locations. 'The Way We Work in 2025 and Beyond' is a PricewaterhouseCoopers survey of over 200 HR professionals from national and international companies based in Switzerland. It identifies key trends in six HR areas and predicts what the workplace might look like in the future. Regarding mobility, the authors write: "Our survey shows that global mobility projects are likely to get shorter, with employees working abroad on assignment for up to three months or a year. Our survey also predicts an increase in the number of 'commuters', employees living and working in different countries." This may well be the case for workforces worldwide.

Business people, humanitarian workers, government staff and many other professions often travel for work. During the research for this book, I also discovered that professional yachtsmen are often away from home too.

There are going to be different frequencies of travel and different reasons for said travel, some of which you will have signed up for, while others may come as a surprise. Your partner may travel Monday to Friday and come home on the weekend, or they may travel two weeks out of every month. Different frequencies of business travel have different challenges and advantages.

Speaking of advantages, one mother in the 'Holding the Fort Abroad Survey' mentions "not having to factor in the partner's routine when they are travelling, which allows for more flexibility". Another says: "The frequent travel also means more miles for airlines and hotels which has meant nicer family vacations," and yet another: "Children have not had to move schools. I have been able to stay in my current job." My favourite is: "Time apart to enjoy the bed to yourself. Variety of experiences to share."

No matter how frequently your partner travels for work, I notice one thing – you live with a suitcase either about to be packed or just unpacked; your partner is transitioning back into your everyday life or transitioning out of it. So that is why, this year, when Olivier is home, we've decided that he'll put his suitcase away between trips. No more open suitcase at the foot of the bed, reminding us that his presence is only temporary.

Work Travel and Life Abroad

A friend took me by surprise one day when she commented that her husband's work travel felt completely different now that they were living abroad.

"When we were living in the USA and Mark was travelling from there," Clare begins, "my family was close by to help if needed. I was a senior manager in a hospital and my life was busy. I didn't really have time to think when he was gone, I had a demanding job, I took care of our daughter and I had many social engagements that kept me occupied and content."

Loss of support network

Clare's observation highlights how living abroad can impact the Accompanying Partner. One mother living in the UK who travels for work writes: "As we live abroad, there is no local family support, so we rely on friends more. If we lived near family, we would have more support and call on them to help rather than only using each other." It is also possible that your friends and family 'back home' won't understand the challenges you are facing and therefore won't know how to support you from afar. One mum I interviewed shared that she once called her parents during a tropical storm on the island where she was working. They told her: "It can't be that bad. Let us know when you are back in your room." She says that it was at that moment she realised her parents, who had supported her so much up to that point, would never understand what some things would mean for her.

The likelihood of long hours and business travel often adds to the feeling of being unsupported that frequently occurs for the Accompanying Partner as they move outside the country they know so well.

One mum shares how she credits her survival during difficult years to an older couple who befriended her, Ted and Susan. "Without Ted, I don't think I would have survived," she says. "He was an angel that just came into my life. He was my absolute and utter support. It felt like he was sent to me. Susan was amazing and she supported our friendship. That first year when my husband started travelling for work because of the Global Financial Crisis, life was incredibly difficult. I believe my husband and I were hanging on by a thread, our marriage shaken by the recent move from Africa to Ireland, his homeland. Had I grown up in Ireland, I'd have had supportive family relations around me and I know things would have been easier. My husband's family were fantastic, but I barely knew them. And I was different – with different ways of doing things."

This mum was fortunate to find a couple who befriended her so wholeheartedly. Another mum reinforces the difficulty in finding support abroad in the 'Holding the Fort Abroad Survey': "Work travel when the whole family is living abroad is different to travel when you are living in one of your home countries. The support system is nearly non-existent, the burden falls on the staying partner. It seems easier for the travelling partner to feel light when the other is holding the fort, dealing with everything, even the tasks that are challenging, be it administrative tasks, education, parenting."

Loss of identity and independence

My heart was racing, my palms getting sweaty as I stood, ashamed, in front of the cashier.

"I'm so sorry, Madam," he repeated for the third time, "we only accept credit cards or cash."

I looked at my purse, my mind furiously trying to find a solution. I didn't have enough cash on me, expenses for the move had been higher than expected and our cash limit for withdrawals was maxed out so I couldn't withdraw more. They wouldn't accept my debit card. Olivier was out of the country on a work-related trip. I didn't have a credit card because my name wasn't on the bank account as I wasn't receiving a steady income. I could see the cashier wondering: Who on earth doesn't have a credit card? I turned around, mumbled my apologies and ran out of the shop, cheeks burning with embarrassment.

Myriam is a mum of two boys. She and her family have lived in Angola, Rwanda, Ecuador and Hungary. She strongly advises deciding on an amount that one partner can spend without consulting the other and for each partner to have access to funds on a credit card.

There have been other times where I have angrily argued with a bank manager because a certain payment needed to be made by a certain date and for that to happen a crucial document needed to be signed, by my husband, of course, who was out of town, again. Sometimes there was no reasoning with bureaucracy.

This increased reliance on your partner is often compounded by having to resign from your own job when the whole family moves. Professional qualifications are not necessarily recognised in the new location, so the loss is felt keenly. After several moves, it may seem the career path is lost forever. Some turn to further education, others to portable businesses.

Some may feel they are dependent in more ways than just financially. They have left their jobs, their personal source of income, sometimes their life's passion, to accompany their partner. They may even be on a 'dependent's visa'. This may mean they are not allowed to work, which may strip them of their sense of purpose. Add to all this a total disorientation and feeling like an idiot every time they try to buy the slightest little thing, or feeling like a child when they don't know which button to press when crossing the road, and you can understand the stresses. Mariam Navaid Ottimofiore, author of *This Messy Mobile Life*, shares: "In Singapore, I was my husband's dependent in every possible way. He was the breadwinner and I had a visa which said 'dependent visa'. I couldn't even call the phone company without them asking to speak to the main account holder. I couldn't change our internet plan without having his okay. I couldn't do anything. How am I supposed to keep day to day life running when I need to go to him every two minutes asking for his permission and asking him to handle it? If your husband is travelling during that time, then you feel it even more."

In 'Lost in the Move Abroad', Robin Pascoe's article for *The Telegraph* in September 2004, the expat author writes: "Ask accompanying expatriate spouses anywhere in the world to identify the most overwhelming loss they feel after moving abroad and identity will likely be the near-unanimous reply."

Increased stress

"Stress is the body's reaction to any change that requires an adjustment or response. It can react to these changes physically, mentally or emotionally," according to the Cleveland Clinic, a nonprofit multispecialty academic medical center. "Stress becomes negative when a person faces continuous challenges without relief or relaxation between stressors."

Warning signs of stress could be dizziness, a general feeling of 'being out of it', general aches and pains, headaches or acid reflux symptoms. You can view the full list and read tips on how to reduce it on the Clinic's website (see *Bibliography: Other Sources*).

It seems only natural then that as we are stressed on a personal level, this stress will overflow into our relationships, notably in our marriages.

In their study 'Managing Stress in the Expatriate Family: A Case Study of the State Department of the United States of America' published in *Public Personnel Management* in March 2010, Amanda Wilkinson and Gangaram Singh write: "There are three major components of stress: uncertainty concerning outcomes, lack of control over situations, and ambiguity concerning expectations. By their very nature, overseas assignments are characterized by uncertainty, lack of control, and ambiguity." They repeat the word 'uncertainty' no less than 15 times!

Uncertainty and lack of control may come from the change in the amount of travel. You may agree to one form of travel which might end up morphing into something completely different.

"The travel estimates are never spot on," says Mariam Ottimofiore, who was for many years the accompanying spouse of a frequent business traveller. "They're never realistic and things change so fluidly. A job you have been told includes 20% to 30% travel could easily end up being 50% travel. Had you been told upfront it would be 50% travel (that's two weeks out of every month), you may have taken different decisions about any extra projects to take on personally. Expectations are key. The challenge, especially in the corporate world, is that a lot of the time, you just don't know. The game keeps changing. And what you had signed up for is not going to be the same reality a year later. How do you then pull out and say this is too hard, when you signed up for it? That is what I found truly difficult because jobs started off with less travel but then ended up being way more travel than we had both anticipated."

The travel estimates are never spot on.

Dr Pauline Boss, author of *Ambiguous Loss: Learning to Live with Unresolved Grief*, coined the term 'ambiguous loss' to describe those who had lost a loved one but had no closure or some combination of presence and absence. "Expat families," she adds, "all have an ambiguous loss – the loss of family friends left behind, perhaps the loss of a home left behind, the loss of the one parent who is traveling or at long days at work."

Vici Tanner is a Certified Expat Life Coach and Founder of the Facebook Group 'Support for Expat Mums Worldwide'. She is also no stranger to living abroad with a travelling spouse. She shares: "When we first moved abroad, we were young, free and single traveling the world for our jobs. Then we got married, had a baby and moved to Bali in 2013 for my husband's job. That's when he started to travel and I had our second child."

She highlights that there will be so many 'extra' challenges an expat parent will be facing on their own: "You might realise your husband will be gone a lot and that you are going to miss him and that you are going to have to care for the kids, but there is obviously so much more to it than that. I've had to lock rats in a room and wait for someone to take care of them in the morning. The thing is it takes longer to find someone. When you are in your home country and something breaks, you know who to call. You call them and they come. But when you are abroad, there is no one around the corner that you can call. I've driven around at night, in a storm, trying to keep the kids cool because the electricity had gone off and the air conditioning wasn't working anymore. I've had to teach my toddler how to access emergency numbers on my phone through my favourites because I am the only adult in the house. If anything happens, she needs to know who to call. There were many trips on my own trying to juggle a baby and a toddler's needs."

Another mum, whose father travelled a lot when she was younger, remembers her mother being in an accident and them sleeping at her teacher's house because no one else was available to take care of them. She highly recommends telling the children where they can access emergency numbers and insurance documents. "This isn't to frighten them," she says, "but if an accident does happen, they will know what to do and won't feel so bewildered."

"As an expat mum," Vici continues, "I didn't want to complain because there are so many mums around the world that have challenges, and I have so much to be grateful for. So I was very stoic. But on the inside, it's really, really, really tough. I want to give tribute to all the expat parents around the world who are doing this."

A Suitcase by the Door

In fact, in her book, *A Great Move,* Katia Vlachos mentions work travel as one of the stressors when arriving in a new location and one of the uncertainties to get a grip on when considering an opportunity abroad. The very first couple she mentions in her introduction were taken by surprise by the amount of business travel involved. It became a major factor in them returning home as they hadn't prepared for that.

Chapter 2
The 'Holding-the-Fort' Partner

"Each of us has that right, that possibility, to invent ourselves daily. If a person does not invent herself, she will be invented. So, to be bodacious enough to invent ourselves is wise."
MAYA ANGELOU

Nyon, Switzerland, 2008

The cold leather digs into my forehead as I hunch over the steering wheel of my car and press my skin on its cooling surface. Our new and firstborn baby is nestled in his car seat and securely strapped in the back. Thankfully, he is settled and has stopped crying. Baby and I are in the underground carpark of the local supermarket in Nyon, the Swiss town where we currently live. We are about to drive home after a shopping trip. Only, we aren't going anywhere. The minute I climb into the front seat, tears start running down my cheeks and sobs wrack my body uncontrollably. It's been happening over the last few days in random places: on the street as I push my baby's stroller, in the bread aisle at the supermarket or at home while I cook dinner or clean up around the house.

A kind, elderly gentleman walking by spots me and hesitantly knocks on the car window.

"Madame, are you all right? Do you need help?" he asks, his voice full of concern and his face peering at me through the glass pane.

I open the window a crack. All I can do is nod and utter a few words.

"Oui. Merci, Monsieur. Tout va bien," I manage through my sobs. "Everything is okay. My husband is in Darfur at the moment."

"Je suis désolé, Madame. I am so sorry. Please take care of yourself."

"Oui, merci beaucoup."

This is all so embarrassing. I would describe myself as a strong, independent woman. I travelled and lived in different countries for 10 years before meeting my husband, Olivier, at the age of 30 and moving to Switzerland.

Why the sudden meltdowns?

As soon as possible, I book an appointment with my local doctor. I really need to get some help with this. That said, how he is going to help remains a mystery to me. Could I be suffering from post-partum depression?

The doctor has a kind face. It is my first time in his office because I haven't registered with a doctor yet. For this appointment, I picked the doctor closest to where we live.

The 'Holding the Fort' Partner

It looks like Dr Ferdinand and his wife share a practice and he happens to be the one taking on new patients.

"Bonjour, Madame. What can I do for you today?" he asks as he shows me to a seat.

"Bonjour, Monsieur. Well, it seems I start crying in random places at random times. I really don't understand what is happening to me."

"I see. Tell me a little bit about yourself."

"Sure," I reply. "About two years ago, I moved to Switzerland to get married. We have a four-month-old son. We moved a week ago to a new house; I also stopped breastfeeding last week and went back to work. My husband works for a humanitarian organisation and travels very often. He is in Darfur at the moment."

Doctor Ferdinand pauses a moment, leans over his desk towards me and gently says, "Don't you think it's a lot for one person?"

Pause.

The silence stretches between us as his words sink into my heart and my brain. Yes, it is a lot to deal with for one person. I am still figuring out what it means to be a mum, in the midst of all these big changes inside and outside my body. My husband is often absent, a suitcase either being packed or being unpacked.

Yes, the doctor is right. This is a lot.

Don't you think it's a lot for one person?

Even though this interaction took place over a decade ago, I will never forget Dr Ferdinand's kindness as he mirrored back to me what I was experiencing. Moving, having a baby, starting a new job and getting married are considered some of the top stressors life has to offer, along with grief, major illness and divorce. I had lived four of those in two years, all with a travelling husband.

Acknowledge Your Feelings

Whether this was your first move or the fifth one, you may have genuinely been happy to move; the decision was taken together, you were up for a challenge, an adventure – even to a new place. You would make new friends and discover new ways of doing things. These discoveries may even have come to pass. Along the way, a few months in, or a few years into a life that turned nomadic, seeds of resentment may have been planted. If you have not felt any bitterness whatsoever towards your partner or your lifestyle, then I suspect you have amazing communication between you, an effective support network that you can debrief with, and that you have mastered tools that help you work through situations that arise that may seem unfair and unjust. Or maybe you are not dealing with it at all and are in denial.

The definition of resentment is bitter indignation (anger and disappointment) at having been treated unfairly.

The 'Holding the Fort' Partner

In his article 'Why Resentment Lasts – and How to Defeat It' for *Psychology Today* in March 2017, Dr Robert Enright points out that resentment can represent "a development in one's anger from mild to deeper – and it lingers. This kind of resentment can lead to unhappiness, continual irritability, and psychological compromise, including excessive anxiety and depression."

If you have experienced, or you are currently experiencing resentment; if you have felt that your partner's career was taking off and yours wasn't, that they were being treated like a VIP when you ended up fetching and carrying for them, know that it is a reaction many Accompanying Partners have had. Robin Pascoe, in her book *A Moveable Marriage: Relocate Your Relationship Without Breaking It*, aptly describes what happens when, usually the wife, suddenly gets asked to take her husband's shirts to the cleaners or to wait for a repair technician. "Many women find this the first seeds of many resentment-filled shocks to come: the realization that once moved, the marriage of equals now has a less-than-equal spouse," she writes. We may have left our jobs, we may feel like we have given up the possibility of finding a job at a future date. Maybe we think that we are not earning or contributing financially to the family, and so we downplay our crucial role in our family's well-being and financial success. I thought like this, I still do sometimes, and I must fight these thoughts.

We downplay our crucial role in our family's well-being and financial success.

This bitterness might get exacerbated, in a globally mobile life, by the constant shifting of what has been agreed. This is a life that has a fair share of uncertainty and changing goalposts. One day, your husband is telling you he will be home every night; a few months later, you find he is gone most of the time. What do you do when there are sudden changes to the conditions you had laid out, had both agreed on and were counting on (by the way, you had even expressed what you would need to be 'okay' at the right time in the right place)? Worse still, in my opinion, is that you don't always see gradual changes coming. Ten, twenty or thirty years after setting off on your international lifestyle, you find yourself living a life far from your ageing parents. You're missing your aunts, uncles, nephews and nieces. Your children have left the nest. You're not sure who you are anymore.

One mother puts it this way: "It sounds quite petty for me to admit being resentful of my partner, yet it was a very real emotion. I knew rationally that he was working to make a living for his family, but part of me, especially when my kids were younger, couldn't help feeling resentful. I even resented the alone time he got on long-haul flights. That for me was part of what I was missing out on too. I would have loved those hours alone. Even though we had made a decision to move and to have children, for me to give up all the life that I had been leading before children, the travel involved, definitely involved some resentment. The only thing that helped was to communicate about it and admit to it when it crept in, instead of negating it. I would say to him, 'Look, I'm feeling resentful. I know it's not fair and I know it's not pretty.' He understood that my feelings, even if he didn't agree with them, were valid and allowed me to express them. I didn't want him to quit his job and stay home. I just wanted to be able to express my frustration and any resentment showing up. It was so important for me to acknowledge that I was having a hard time and that I just needed to talk about it. A plan as to how you can get some more freedom when he's back can definitely help. I always used to joke that as soon as he walked in the door, I'd welcome him home, acknowledge he was probably exhausted from a 20-hour flight or a trip, and then tell him I was exhausted and off to the spa! Although in fairness, and to keep things fun, we had this game that whoever was getting less sleep, 'won' rest time."

My mother's story illustrates how, sometimes, life choices lead you onto paths you may end up resenting. She leaves her home country in her early twenties as a vibrant, feisty young lady who very much knows her own mind (still does). Ten years later, in Lebanon, she meets my dad and agrees to marry him on condition they continue to live in the Middle East. My Welsh father, as much in love with that part of the world as he is smitten with my mum, readily agrees. He has lived in Jordan and has already started learning Arabic with a view to moving there. After a few years in Lebanon, the Civil War starts. For a variety of reasons, including the fact that they have friends and work colleagues moving to France, my parents decide to settle in Orange, a small town in Provence. Here begins an extremely difficult time for my mum. She has two young children and no knowledge of the language. She recalls a time when she was in the local pharmacy, needing to pick up medicine for me or my brother. The pharmacist in charge, knowing full well my mother could not speak any French, that she was fairly new to the area, and being himself fully capable of speaking English, flatly refused to help her with her request and insisted she fumble through. She did eventually learn how to speak French and made many friends in Orange, but it took years for her to accept that she wasn't going back to Lebanon. She said that for an entire year, she refused to learn the French language.

Growing up, I would tell her it was a question of attitude. If only she could change her attitude about not being in the region of the world she wanted to live in, then maybe she wouldn't be so depressed. Little did I know that a number of years later, I would find myself with two young children (eerily at the same age my mother moved to France, with children the exact same age), in a country where I didn't speak the language, at a doctor's office where I couldn't express what was wrong with my child. All of a sudden, forcing myself to change my attitude didn't seem quite as easy as I'd suggested.

Granted, my father was practically always at home. He had an office in town but as he was his own boss, he would often run errands with my mum and spend time with us kids.

Loneliness can be devastating when moving abroad, and travelling for business could well turn out to be a big part of your partner's assignment.

"Due to the hours they work and the stress they're under you will be alone a lot. My husband was constantly travelling leaving me alone in Singapore for weeks on end. I got lonely and missed my relationship with him," shares a blogger who writes under the name Character 32.

The Founder of Interval Coaching, Carolyn Parse Rizzo, recounts how the early years of living as a 'lovepat' were not easy: "I was the main breadwinner at the beginning of our marriage, then I left my job when my husband got a job farther north. We had a new baby; and that summer my husband thought it would be best for me and the baby to stay at our house in the country where it was cooler. Everyone in my little support system was at least one hour away. My husband was two hours away. I was sleep deprived, lonely, and I felt bad about myself because I was not living up to my own expectations of being a mother. I became really creative finding ways to not be alone. It would have been better if I had asked for what I needed. The thing is, I didn't know what I needed."

Needs and feelings are interconnected but Dr Steven Stosny, in his article 'The Curse of Emotional Needs' published in *Psychology Today* in July 2019, warns us that feelings could be showing us a *perceived* need: "Most painful conflicts in relationships begin with one partner making an emotional demand, motivated by a perceived 'need', which the other, motivated by a different 'need', regards as unfair." The trick is to identify our feelings – loneliness, jealousy, bitterness, anger, grief – and to take responsibility for getting our needs met.

"Embrace your feelings," advises Béatrice de Carpentier, Marriage and Family Counsellor for the Expat Communication Academy, "otherwise they may find an unhealthier way of being expressed. It is vital to respond kindly to yourself as you acknowledge them. Ask yourself what this situation brings up for you from your past. Memories of loss or a separation could be creating anxiety."

Karen tells me her story of how she and Tom moved from South Africa to Ireland with their blended family in 2005. In 2007, anticipating the looming economic crisis, her husband ends his project in Ireland and starts working abroad on various construction developments. Her story, although unique in its details and circumstances, has flavours of other women I have interviewed who have shared with me their own experience of living in a country they were not raised in and having a travelling husband.

"I was tetchy when he said he needed to start working away from home," she shares. "I was still a relative newcomer in Ireland. The only other time I had been there was for a week for a family wedding. I knew nobody and he was about to leave. We had just moved out of the temporary housing we had been in and into a lovely family home we had fallen in love with. I was alone with six children under 10, including a baby of four months. But we didn't have a choice. My husband told me that if he didn't find work then, he would have to go further away at a later date. I was angry, resentful, and miserable when he said that to me. I felt trapped and bitter. This wasn't how it was meant to be. Our lovely home suddenly felt like a noose around my neck. I remember crying a lot and wondering how I would manage half a dozen children and a home alone in a new country. I spent many nights awake trying to clear the fuzz from my head. I began searching for 'tools' that were going to help me mentally and spiritually."

I knew nobody and he was about to leave.

2010 was a turning point in Karen's life. With another baby on the way, she began Parelli Natural Horsemanship with a friend in order to deepen her understanding of horses and complement her lifelong love of horses. She explains, "It was not an easy journey. It took time to learn from the innate behaviour of the horse – a prey animal – how our human (predator) emotions are more often than not out of control. The horse could tell if I hadn't completely dealt with a negative emotion even though I thought I had. The experience was uncomfortable at first. Life seemed easier before, but to take a journey such as this is so worth it. My life changed in ways I couldn't have imagined. This change in me began to alter for the better my relationship with self, my husband, my children and our whole family dynamic began to flourish despite our challenges." Karen suggests finding the tools that enhance our emotional fitness.

Jealousy is another feeling that could come knocking at our door as our partner travels while we are home. Our international life has enabled us to travel as a family, for which I am so grateful, but I am still seriously jealous of where he travels. He has visited the pyramids in Egypt and swum in the Dead Sea in Israel. He has travelled on the bullet train in Japan and slept in a traditional *ryokan* (which, ironically, I booked for him). Generally, though, I always encourage him to stay a few nights extra after the meetings are over, in order to leave the hotel and see the sights.

Travel may not be the thing that makes you feel you are missing out. There may be other things you think your partner has the freedom to do, like further personal or professional development to name but two, while you carry the main responsibility for the day-to-day running of the home. Writing a bucket list might be helpful. It is also important to be vulnerable about what we feel we are missing out on. Are there other ways of filling those desires?

I'm writing my bucket list so that I have my own places I aim to visit. I wouldn't want them to get forgotten in the frantic pace of life! They are also good reminders of trips we can take together in the future.

"Feelings are meant to be felt," says my therapist.

"But I am afraid that I will drown in them if I let myself feel," I reply.

"When you allow yourself to feel them, they will shift. That's the incredible thing about feelings."

I am encouraged that a 'holding the fort' expat partner is not condemned to a lifetime of negative feelings.

> I am encouraged that a
> 'holding the fort' expat partner
> is not condemned to a lifetime
> of negative feelings.

Vici Tanner warns about comparing to 'back home'. "When you are tired, you can be in a frame of mind that doesn't enable you to see clearly," she says. "You may start thinking about how amazing it was in your home country. That's the thing though, you only remember the good."

Take Responsibility for Your Needs

"Assertiveness allows for the confident expression of your needs and feelings without the need for proof. Being assertive means expressing your wants while being mindful of the opinions, feelings and wants of others."
JUDY MURPHY

Judy Murphy has sold over 100,000 copies of her book *Assertiveness: How to Stand Up for Yourself and Still Win the Respect of Others*. In the context of global mobility, where shifts in wants and needs happen frequently, no doubt exacerbated when a partner often travels for work, being assertive is going to go a long way to making sure the needs of each family member are balanced and attended to as much as possible, including your own.

The concept of the 'Losing Triangle' (also known as the 'Drama Triangle') developed by psychiatrist Dr Stephen Karpman, is something I have learned during my therapy sessions and has proved an extremely valuable tool in helping me understand how to be more assertive and to avoid running around trying to cater to everyone else's needs while expressing my own clearly. Allow me to unpack this a little...

Imagine a triangle with its three corners. Each corner can be a behaviour we choose, a role we play, when we have needs.

In the Drama Triangle, one corner is where the Victim role resides. If we spend time here, we tend to bemoan the fact that our needs aren't being met and that no one is noticing. I can easily slip into the Victim role if I am not careful.

The second corner represents the Rescuer role, always wanting to meet the needs of others, to the extent of overstepping into things for which we are not responsible.

The third corner represents what is called the Persecutor. When our needs aren't met, we may become angry or resentful. We may want to punish whoever we think should have met our needs.

The 'Holding the Fort' Partner

These roles are also interconnected so your partner may become the Persecutor when you feel like the Victim and you can look for a Rescuer in a family member or another romantic relationship, for example, with the risks that go with that.

You can read more about this triangle in Dr Karpman's book, *A Game Free Life*.

Acey Choy presents the Winning Triangle in the *Transactional Analysis Journal* in 1990. This triangle also represents different ways of behaving for our needs to be met but with a considerable mindset shift. Instead of being a Victim, we become Vulnerable, aware of the needs that we have and open to expressing them. The Rescuer becomes the Carer, expressing concern and care for the needs of others but also awareness of their responsibilities and the healthy boundaries of caring for someone else. Lastly, the Persecutor becomes Assertive, saying words like: "These are my needs, and I will take responsibility to find creative ways to get them met."

Carolyn Parse Rizzo shares how she took matters into her own hands: "My husband was home on the weekends but had hurt his back and couldn't do much; he couldn't even pick up our toddler. I felt so confined. Then I asked myself: *What am I missing? How can I create a sensation of my free-est moments?* So, I set up a campfire. Then I thought: *I need a hammock to relax in.* I got a hammock. I stopped blaming him for all the things I couldn't have or do and asked myself what I could do. I flattened a piece of earth, put a tent up in the back yard and took my son camping."

According to the Mayo Clinic's article entitled 'Being assertive: Reduce stress, communicate better' published on their website in May 2020: "Assertiveness is a communication style." The authors advise starting small, in situations where the risks are low, keeping emotions in check, practising saying no and using 'I' statements so others know what we are saying. For example, saying 'I think' rather than 'you're wrong'.

Vici Tanner is passionate about supporting mums emotionally and socially rather than the parenting side of things. She explains: "If I had known years ago what I know now about being self-aware and being kinder to myself when I needed to be, I think it would have been easier. As we are alone so much of the time, we also need to be able to deal with our feelings alone and the only way I know how is to be self-aware and emotionally resilient. You've got to be aware of what is causing the frustration, or anger. Most of the time, in my opinion, it's not because your partner is away. I think it's because you're tired or you're not feeling well or the children have frustrated you or you've had to clear up after the dog. But because we are frustrated, we blame the travel. I need to know where my feelings are coming from. And the fact that I do makes a massive, massive difference to my life. Once you can get a handle on what your emotions are and figure out what's going on, then you can find solutions; for example, more rest or talking to somebody. Many expat women that I've spoken to wish they could be sure that they were doing things right, that they had family around to talk to and bounce ideas off. Being out of our home country means that we don't have the culture around us that's the same as we had growing up. Once you have figured out why you are feeling what you are, you can be confident in your choices that you make moving forward."

Identify your needs

"The process of identifying your NEEDS! involves peeling away the layers of the onion of the unhappiness and dissatisfaction in your life."
JIM TAYLOR

Taking care of personal needs takes time. I used to devote about one per cent of my time to self-care, if that. My thirties felt like I was on a fast train. It felt like I couldn't stop and get off: taking care of children, of the house, working, volunteering, packing and unpacking my husband's suitcase, laundry, cooking, cleaning. Until I got very sick and had to stop working outside the home.

For a few years now, I have been careful to increase the time I take care of myself but it is still nowhere near what it should be to really hit the spot. And I regularly have to take stock and recognise the signs of when this area of my life is slipping.

The 'Self-Nurture Survey', part of The Thymes Limited's *Take Thymes for Yourself* public awareness campaign, was created in partnership with Dr Alice Domar, author of the best-seller *Self Nurture: Learning to Care For Yourself as Effectively As You Care For Everyone Else* and Director of Harvard's Mind/Body Center for Women's

Health. Of 1,000 women surveyed across the USA, 80% saw the value of doing something for themselves, only 2% considered self-care selfish but only a third spent 30 minutes or less doing nurturing activities just for themselves.

Re-evaluating your situation is vital as needs will vary depending on circumstances. Different stages of life may highlight the changes but don't take that for granted and do not forget to re-evaluate and move priorities around if needed.

Need for time

You may be flicking through this book and thinking, *Where on earth do I find the time to read this, let alone do anything for myself?*

Let me walk you through a few tricks that might help you reclaim some time.

One highly effective way of redeeming the time is to make one errand, or one chore, or anything really that you have to do, work for you. What I mean by that is simply this: if you need to run an errand, go to the nearby park for that five-minute breather you have been promising yourself. At the very end, tag on that difficult phone conversation you have been dreading (or do that first, then take a breather). Either way, for one errand, you have ticked three items off your to-do list.

See how many things you can group together to do at the same time, or that would serve more than one purpose. Another example: your son needs outdoor activities, you need to do something enjoyable. What do you both enjoy that you could do together?

Here's another example: I had been meaning to send a care parcel to my husband. It was starting to get embarrassing because his former work colleagues were sending him chocolate, cheese and all sorts of goodies but he wasn't getting a parcel from his wife. I gave it some thought... how many purposes can this parcel-sending fulfil? So, this is what I did:

- I got our eldest to design and print the recipient and sender stickers. That was a double whammy because it was an activity for him and he was learning a life skill.
- I set up a box with cardboard boxes, the stickers, Sellotape and scissors. Hey presto. Next time I send him a parcel, I have all that is needed right there.

Another way of reclaiming time is to increase the efficiency of your tasks.

Take a step back from your day and consider one thing that is taking you a ridiculous amount of time. That's where you want to start streamlining. For example, I was taking a huge amount of time deciding on menus for the week. Some families just have the same meal on the same day of the week every week. That doesn't really work in our family, so I devise menus every week. Well, that took so much time, and the boys ended up complaining anyway. I bought a chart with the days of the week on it, drew up a list of the main meals and evening meals that we usually had. Now the boys fill out the chart every week as they pick from the list. Job done, in a fraction of the time.

An especially useful book I have found is *Organizing Solutions for People With ADHD: Tips and Tools to Help You Take Charge of Your Life and Get Organized* by Susan Pinsky. No need to have Attention Deficit Hyperactivity Disorder or a cluttered household to find ideas in this book that may help you reclaim time. This book is an absolute lifesaver. The ideas are straightforward and most importantly, feasible. "It turns out," Susan Pinsky writes, "that any home that struggles with organization, whether because of illness, lack of time, multiple children, working parents, tight space, excess clutter, or an overcommitted schedule (*or 'a solo parent with a partner working away from home', I might add here*), should rely on a system that gets the job things done efficiently, with the least amount of time and work put in."

Susan Pinsky recommends using a simple one-calendar system, for example, and then to learn how to reduce your commitments. She works her way through each room of the house, suggesting efficient changes that will help any busy parent to make household chores more efficient. She suggests, for example, getting radical with family laundry with the Laundry Day system, when "everyone takes their laundry basket-style hamper to the laundry room" and an adult cycles each person's load through the machine on a neutral setting. Each person returns the basket of their single load to their room and folds and puts away their own laundry. If the whole family does it at the same time, it will help 'lend focus' to the task. Another option is the Daily Laundry system, when one day of the week is scheduled for each family member's laundry. "Each member is responsible for toting his or her hamper to the laundry area the morning of Laundry Day (or even the night before) and dumping the whole thing into the wash as a single load. During the day, if assistance is needed, an adult can switch the load into the dryer. By evening, the owner should return the single load of clean laundry to his or her bedroom, fold and put away."

It does not have to be a household chore; it could be something you do for work. Start with one thing, then move on to another task that takes more time than necessary.

Another area that slapped me in the face when I was considering where my time went comes from a hidden source: other people's expectations. These people might not even be a part of your life anymore or have any authority over it, yet their expectations still have a hold on you. I am someone who can stand a little bit of mess around the house but I was always doing housework to my mother's (very high) standard rather than my own. It took me a while to realise what I was doing and to release myself of that expectation. It is amazing how much freedom can be in that.

Yet another area that bears thinking about. Take a step back and take a 'big picture look' at your life. Are you doing something for someone else that they should be doing themselves? This is often the case when we do things for our children that they should actually be doing themselves. This could take time to set up as you show your children and teach them but it will save time in the long run. Again, just choose one area to work on first.

Need for help

"It shouldn't hurt your ego," shares Mariam Ottimofiore, when describing her journey to asking for help. "It took me many years to get this right," she continues. "In Singapore I had my first child and I never asked anybody for help. My husband was looking after the whole of Southeast Asia for work. He was in New Zealand one day, Australia the next, the Philippines and Malaysia, you name it. I just said to him, "It doesn't matter if you're in Jakarta, I've got this." I was working part-time initially and then full-time, but it was really tough. You realise very quickly how much you can do. You know, nobody gives you a gold medal at the end of the day. You do have a choice. Looking back, I should've gotten some help because I was definitely drowning and trying to do it all, which never worked." She points out the difference in the stigma attached to having help. In certain countries, we are 'conditioned' to believe the woman should do it all by herself; in others, hiring help in the home is expected. She goes on to explain that as an expat partner or spouse, we feel it a lot more because we may have already lost our identity, our sense of self, our career. We think, *I've lost so many things that in the end, if I outsource even this, then what is left for me?* It feels like just another thing that is being taken away from you. We feel more vulnerable, even if we know what it is like to move. This may be our 'only' responsibility, and we may fear a sense of failure that we can't 'even do that'.

It is vital here to remind ourselves that we are all different. One person may need a full-time cleaner and childcare while others not. What helps one person may not be helpful for another. It depends what you are used to, what you grew up with, what society tells you that you should be doing. Not all expats are equal nor face the exact same challenges. There are some similarities, true, but if your partner is travelling a lot, then comparing how you are living with someone whose partner doesn't travel as much isn't fair: the extra time and effort you are putting into communicating in your long-distance relationship (and including them in parenting) is time others may be spending resting or studying.

People who have grown up where you are living might feel like they are managing everything on their own and so should you, but they are not expats. "They're in their comfort zone, they speak the language, they know where to go to lodge a complaint," reminds Mariam. "They get around bureaucracy. They can make a dentist appointment without needing to prepare themselves for thirty minutes to do it in a foreign language that they don't feel comfortable speaking. They know all the grocery stores; they know who to call in an emergency. They have that environment; they have that support system. We, as expats, built everything up from scratch."

It shouldn't hurt your ego to ask for help.

You may want to look at various areas, not just the 'obvious' ones like cleaning and childcare. Start building a support team around you. You don't even need the whole team in place to benefit from a little help.

- **Virtual Assistance** for any administrative support, be it for home or for work.
- **Emotional support**. Ask yourself who cheers you up the most. Ask them to call you on a regular basis so that you don't need to be proactive when you are potentially at your most vulnerable and least likely to reach out. Also brainstorm how you can include rest, what activities are restorative and not just escapism (although, I must admit, escaping my reality sometimes re-energises me). If someone is giving out a lot of themselves, they also need to be replenished. The input part of my emotional 'cup' is no longer flowing. Focus on what fills your emotional bank account.
- **Call a professional**. You may want to put in place a regular call to a Psychotherapist or now may be a good time to hire a Certified Life Coach. They will help you make sense of patterns of behaviour.
- **Practical help**. Difficulty in finding childcare is often the topmost complaint I see on social media posts from overwhelmed mums. This is real, especially for the globally mobile. The main thing I have learnt is to find other ways of relieving the practical overload. I recently admitted that during

the summer of 2020, the boys and I ate off paper plates. This meant less dishwashing; I could sit instead and drink a coffee. Not necessarily elegant but it provided breathing space. Look at what tedious jobs you can release. For me, this would be laundry, changing the beds, cleaning, cooking/ baking. It does not have to be about the home. There may be aspects of your professional life that you can release or delegate.

- **Family chores**. Is it time for the kids to step up on chores? Can they cook one of the meals? Can they fill out a meal planning calendar from a set list of meals? We dedicate Saturday mornings to work around the house.
- **Co-parent** as much as you can. Be creative. Can your partner have a regular time for playing a game online with the kids? Can they help you with an admin task or keep track of children's chores? Are there decisions regarding the children that can be deferred so that you can take decisions as a couple? How can your partner participate in parenting right now?

Carolyn Parse Rizzo recommends www.workaway.info. It is an online platform that allows people who want to swap their services for room and board in another country to connect with people who need help.

Hiring help was something Colleen, a mum I interviewed, really struggled with when she had young children: "I grew up in a house where we would never hire for anything. We would always do everything ourselves and so it did not feel legitimate to me to pay for it. If it was for childcare, it would only be justified if I was working and making money. But now I do hire help for my own emotional health. It makes you a better mother because you are not resenting being with the children all the time."

You may find that your extended family and friends don't understand why your husband, wife or partner works away from family and they might offer all sorts of unrealistic advice. Even to the point of telling you what you should do and what 'help' you should get. One mum I spoke to shared how her family would immediately ask if she was 'coming home' or if she and her husband were separating, if ever she called to 'vent'.

"Don't discount support from distance grandparents and extended family," encourages Helen Ellis, a distance grandmother herself. She is writing a series of three books, one about each generation of distance families: *Being a Distance Grandparent*, *Being a Distance Son or Daughter*, and *Being a Distance Grandchild*. Her aim is to promote understanding and empathy between all members of distance families. "If children are old enough," she suggests, "once a month, for example, they could have a duty/job/privilege to set up a one-on-one video call or write a letter to their distance grandparent/s. This lessens the burden for the solo parent and alone time with grandparents (or any other distance relative) builds special bonds."

I decided to find a Psychotherapist for myself, someone who was not only a trained professional but who also specialised in dealing with issues stemming from global mobility, travelling partners and multicultural lifestyles. Not only did I need to unburden and speak to someone who would understand, I also needed someone who would recognise patterns of behaviours to help me (and as an extension our family) live in a healthy way, both in our relationships and mentally. She is someone I can speak to about anything, without worrying about compromising relationships by sharing personal information. I specifically chose someone who has been in my shoes. She understands my reality without question but can also identify the mechanisms unfolding from our specific lifestyle and provide the tools I need. The only other people who really understand are my international friends who are experiencing the same things. Those relationships are precious.

Need for fun

"Even though you're growing up, you should never stop having fun."
NINA DOBREV

Adult colouring books are all the rage at the moment. If you are so inclined, buy yourself *The Fun and Relaxing Adult Activity Book: With Easy Puzzles, Coloring Pages, Writing Activities, Brain Games and Much More.* I watch stand-up comedy from time to time and am tempted to set myself a calendar reminder to block off time to laugh out loud.

The National Institute for Play is a non-profit organisation that seeks to promote all that is done for its own sake, all that is voluntary, pleasurable, non-repetitive, and produces a sense of unlocking "the human potential through play in all stages of life using science to discover all that play has to teach us about transforming our world." Dr Stuart Brown, founder of the Institute, defines play as: "Something of well-being, it's flavored by culture, altered to some degree by temperament and gender, it's a fundamental survival drive that comes out of the deepest centers of our brain and fuels action and activity. When you don't get it, as an animal or a human, you pay consequences socially, physically, emotionally, cognitively." In his YouTube video interview by The University of Minnesota's Bakken Center for Spirituality and Healing (uploaded on May 23 2011), Dr Brown talks about how to play as an adult. He stresses that it is best to start with your own play history and to work out what evokes joy and pleasure for oneself, then to honour that throughout our life.

One mother living in Indonesia with children under 10 and whose husband travels two to three weeks regularly, advises anyone holding the fort to: "Make sure you have your own life – when your partner is away a lot, your life can't just be your children and work. You need balance and release as well – dinners or coffees with friends, time at the gym and so on."

A mum living in Switzerland, whose husband travels two to three days per week suggests: "Remember that the person staying home is not eating out, sleeping in a quiet hotel room or getting to see new places. Be sure to allow for the non-traveling partner to have their own mini breaks away."

I have only listed here three needs – time, help and fun. Needs are personal to each person. Vici Tanner has shared how, despite not being an exercise person, physical activity has dragged her out of the pits of despair time and time again. For many, exercise is a definite need rather than a nice-to-have.

Self-care on the go

I launched a challenge on Facebook asking people to help me collate ideas for self-care 'on the go'. Sometimes we can carve out a time for a morning meditation or walk, but it can also be useful to drip-feed ourselves what we need.

Here are some of the suggestions received:

- A five-minute tea break in the garden to enjoy the sunshine.
- Breathe in for four seconds, hold for four, breathe out for four.
- Take a few seconds to put on some of your favourite hand cream. Breathe in the scent.
- Put on a calming playlist when you are driving around, not the noisy radio.
- Put a lemon slice in your water bottle and enjoy sipping infused water throughout the day. Keeping hydrated is key.

- Have an audiobook that is an easy listen on demand. Nothing too 'mind-demanding', just something you can relax into. This gives your mind a break as it is familiar and soothing and helps you relax...
- Just walk and enjoy nature.

Count yourself in

"Mummy, you bought strawberries!" shouts our six-year-old from across the room as soon as he sees the red berries peeking out of my shopping bag.

"I have indeed," I reply, smiling at his excitement and ruffling his hair as he zooms past. I know the boys will be over the moon. They love all spring and summer berries.

The strawberries are vibrantly red; I can tell they will be juicy. Sometimes they are picked too early and end up tasting like cardboard, but these must have been left to ripen on the plant.

I set up a bowl for my husband on the kitchen counter, then a bowl for each boy. As I start cutting the strawberries, I make sure that each family member has an equal share.

As I admire the bowls, a thought strikes me. Where is my bowl?

I haven't counted myself in the treat.

That day brought home to me the countless times I had

not taken my needs into account in our various moves and my husband's numerous travels. With hindsight now, I see it was probably a way of escaping the negative feelings that were plaguing me at the time: loneliness, anger, resentment. If I discounted myself, then maybe those feelings wouldn't be real and I wouldn't have to face them. Counting yourself in is a key mindset shift for taking your feelings and needs into account.

One of the ways to identify needs is to know where your vulnerabilities lie.

For me, this was evenings. Once the children had gone to bed, I knew I had difficulty sleeping. I would end up working late until the early hours of the morning or binge watch TV. If I didn't fill those evenings, the lonely feeling would just seep through. It's funny though because there is no way I was lacking friendships and people around me. They just weren't around in the evening. During one of my therapy sessions, the question came up: "Is it because you miss Olivier or because you don't want to be alone?" Although I missed him a lot, I must admit that it was being alone that bothered me. My days were full of meeting people, my kids were always around. How on earth could I feel lonely? Surely those evening hours were my me-time. Maybe it comes from being an extrovert. For an introvert, the vulnerabilities will lie elsewhere. Now that I know that evenings can bring out negative emotions, I am more mindful of what I use them for. Choosing alone time in the evenings becomes more of a conscious decision. Some mothers have shared online that they are scared in the evenings when they are alone with the children. I must admit this was also the case for me. Some installed more alarms, and one even mentioned always having the car keys handy so she could activate the alarm if necessary. We bought cats. It's amazing how a pet's presence can be reassuring.

Celebrate Your Successes

Celebrating small successes is powerful because it helps us to keep going on long projects and in difficult circumstances. Holding the fort abroad qualifies as a long family project!

Teresa Amabile and Steven J Kramer, authors of 'The Power of Small Wins', published in the *Harvard Business Review* in May 2011, analysed diaries of knowledge workers (Programmers, Physicians, Pharmacists, Architects, Engineers, Scientists). They write: "Of all the things that can boost emotions, motivation, and perceptions during a workday, the single most important is making progress in meaningful work. And the more frequently people experience that sense of progress, the more likely they are to be creatively productive in the long run [...] everyday progress – even a small win – can make all the difference in how they feel and perform."

Make a habit of celebrating your successes, no matter how small. Reaching the end of a day of solo parenting is an achievement. Have spontaneous moments when you pat yourself on the back and tell yourself, *Well done,* and schedule in some more planned time, like reaching the end of a week or a milestone. Annabelle, founder of the blog 'the piri-piri lexicon' shares: "I kept a list of everything I did while he was away so that at my low points, I could see what I had achieved."

Know Your Values

"Self-awareness is the ability to see ourselves clearly, to understand who we are, how others see us, and how we fit into the world. Self-awareness gives us power."
TASHA EURICH

Dr Sherry Hamby is Director of the Life Paths Research Center (LPRC) and Founder of ResilienceCon. She is also a Licensed Clinical Psychologist and Research Professor of Psychology at the University of the South. In 2015, she partnered with Dr Victoria Banyard of the University of New Hampshire and Dr John Grych of Marquette University to study the outcomes of the Laws of Life Essay Program where students write down life events as they happen. On top of benefits such as realising that you are helping others, finding your voice and finding a sense of peace, the researchers discovered that writing down your stories had another surprising effect: reaffirming your values. There is a toolkit which you can use to write your own Life Essay if you wish (see *Resources*).

In *The SAGE Handbook of Coaching* (2016), Dr Reinhard Stelter explains that values "connect our actions to our convictions. A value implies the capacity to act and grasps our implicit readiness to do things in a way that is in concordance with our experience, knowledge and beliefs." In other words, what we do springs from our deepest convictions and what is most important to us. As we record our stories, we can trace our reactions back to our values. It is important to remember that some of these may be learned instead of what we believe now. Identifying values is also something that a Life Coach can help you do as a first step to building a future that aligns with those values.

Know what is important to you

Moving overseas, adapting to new ways of doing things, having a partner who is often absent because of work commitments, and the constant changes that a global life brings makes it all the more important to know what you value. Different cultures will emphasise different individual and family traits that they deem vital. "Cultural values are the core principles and ideals upon which an entire community exists," explains Juli Yelnick in 'Cultural Values: Definition, Examples and Importance', a course on www.study.com.

Values could be, for example:

- Dependability
- Reliability
- Loyalty
- Commitment
- Open-mindedness
- Consistency
- Honesty
- Efficiency

- Innovation
- Creativity
- Good humour
- Compassion

- Spirit of adventure
- Motivation
- Positivity

So not only do the values of individual people differ, so do those of whole communities. If you know what you value, you will better understand why you are upset when it is disregarded, and you will be better able to decide how many measures to put in place to protect it. Individualism and collectivism are examples of two cultural values. In the former, the person as an individual is most important. In the latter, family and community come before personal happiness and fulfilment.

As much as coming to a realisation of what you are truly feeling, knowing what is important to you and what you need to function well will lead to greater confidence and knowledge of your identity. This, in turn, leads to being able to act when you have no control over outside circumstances – your partner's irregular travel schedule, for example.

Keep Growing

For years you may have supported your partner in their career, transitioning yourself and your entire family into new countries and new cultures. A feat in itself! You have dealt with home emergencies on your own (probably in a foreign language) and gone alone to parties when your partner was halfway across the world. You created a home and put roots down, no matter for how long. You comforted the children during the umpteenth goodbye, alone, again.

But you may be longing for a career of your own, a space where your dreams, passions and gifts can make an impact. It may be a passion you would like to pursue without it necessarily turning into a ladder-climbing profession. You may be wondering what you would like to do when the children leave the nest and fly away to their own adventures. You may have had plans that had to be put on hold because the next move was coming up and because you were not allowed to work in the country of your partner's next assignment.

Annabelle offers encouragement from her own experience: "Working on personal projects helped me a lot. Even if it is just five minutes, it can make a difference. This is your life, *you* have to make it work." There may not be a way back to your former career path but there is always a way forward. This is your opportunity! And your partner's many work absences cannot stop you from growing on a personal and professional level, even if it is just planting 'seeds' to see what grows.

There may not be a way back to your former career path but there is always a way forward. This is your opportunity!

Invest in yourself

"Be patient with yourself. Self-growth is tender; it's holy ground. There's no greater investment."
STEPHEN R COVEY

Stephen R Covey, in his book *The 7 Habits of Highly Effective People*, speaks about the difference between two Circles. This is a concept that changed my life.

The Circle of Concern encompasses all the areas in life that we worry about but can do absolutely nothing about. He writes that focusing on the Circle of Concern "results in blaming and accusing attitudes, reactive language, and increased feelings of victimization." Speaking of people who focus their attention on this Circle, he writes: "The negative energy generated by that focus, combined with neglect in areas they could do something about, causes their Circle of Influence to shrink." He recommends we focus our efforts and attention on our Circle of Influence, the places in our lives where we already have an impact (or could have one). I have found that the areas I can have an influence on are the ones I can work (and grow) within, which, in turn, has led me to working in what I am passionate about. Does that make sense?

Plant seeds

If you do not have much time, capacity or physical strength (the children are still young, you are suffering from an illness, there is simply no time), you may want to start by planting SEEDS. This has the advantage of being flexible and expanding as children grow older and time permits.

Start with something, then move on to the next step as you work your way through the acronym S.E.E.D.S.

Start with something. Just pick one thing. Do what you seem most attracted to and where you can be proactive: volunteer at the Women's Club, join the PTA, take a class, do anything available that you might enjoy. Go where your interest is awoken. This is not about just 'doing something, anything, just to keep busy'. This is about taking a first step towards investing in yourself for the future. Make sure your involvement is on a trial basis so you have the opportunity to change direction.

Explore new roles, push your limits. Once you have started with something, expand into it. If you joined a local expat group, offer to speak at one of their events. If you have joined the Parent Teacher Association at your child's school, manage a project from start to finish. This is the opportunity to try!

Eliminate the activities that are not thriving. After Starting and Exploring, comes the time to make a few choices. Notice what is growing the most, where you are getting the most fulfilment, and where you are getting positive feedback and having an impact. Go ahead with those.

Dig deeper into activities and roles that are the most promising. Ask your co-workers and other volunteers to give you specific feedback. Start investigating possible training. Look into how the skills that you have and those that you may need can be developed.

Strategise. You may now be in a position to have a 5- or 10-year personal plan that you can turn into a Personal Development Plan. You can use it for your professional life, to grow a set of skills or simply to invest in developing as a person.

"Growth doesn't just happen."
JOHN C MAXWELL

Colleen Higgs signed up to an online course on 'How to write your own book' at 3 am one morning! She just needed something that had nothing to do with motherhood or breastfeeding! It turned out, it wasn't the right thing for her, but it led her to what she is doing today, writing her own blog (www.colleenhiggs.com).

A personal development plan

"I find it fascinating that most people plan their vacations with better care than they plan their lives. Perhaps that is because escape is easier than change."
JIM ROHN

If you find that you have a little more time, or your S.E.E.D.S. have produced results, you may want to start looking at a Personal Development Plan (PDP). It doesn't have to be anything fancy or complicated. I have created a very simple PDP Template as a starting point (see *Appendix 3*). If you have more time and you so desire, you can find resources that suit you to make a more detailed plan.

Achievements
What you want to include is a list of your professional, educational and personal achievements. Are you comfortable speaking in public? Are you a networker? Ask five or so friends to write down what skills and abilities they see in you (ask them for an example).

Vision
Write down where you see yourself in five years. Not necessarily which country, because that may not be possible to predict, but what kind of activities you would want to do, what kinds of people you would like to be working with. You could even write an 'ideal day at work' scenario.

New skills
It is quite likely that to get from where you are now to where you would love to be will mean acquiring new skills. This plan may include training. As Accompanying Partners, especially if we have been out of work for a while, it may be hard for us to invest financially in ourselves.

The 'Holding the Fort' Partner

Your PDP doesn't have to include a financial investment, but if it does you may be thinking, *I am not earning, how can I spend family money on training, a coach or a course?* Remember, investing in professional development is something your employer would be doing if you were working for a company. Your personal development goals would be reviewed and adjusted once a year, at a very minimum, during your appraisal. This plan can easily get put aside and forgotten for parents raising children and who do not have an employer. This is the time to become your own manager.

If you are still hesitating, Amy Modglin advises in her article 'Why You Should Invest in Yourself' in *Forbes* in January 2020 that we ask ourselves these three questions:

1. What will happen if I do not invest in myself?
2. Where will I be in five years if I just wait for growth to happen?
3. How will I get where I want to go if I choose not to invest in myself?

"Believing and investing in yourself is the best way to shift your thinking from a paradigm of excuses to one of solutions."
FARSHAD ASL

You may want to invest in a Certified Life Coach, who will be able to guide you through this process. Architecture is a useful way of looking at coaching, a way of designing and building your future.

This is the time to become your
own manager.

A life balance survey

This is an exercise that we do in coaching. It is about taking a snapshot of where you are at in different areas of life, such as Career, Friendships, Financial Stability and so on. You grade each life area from 1–10, 1 being 'I am not at all satisfied' and 10 being 'I am very happy with the way things are'. In the areas with high scores, you can ask yourself what is particularly working. This may be useful as applied to areas you want to improve. A few months later, as you reassess each area of your life, you can evaluate where you have made progress. I have adapted the 'Life Balance Survey' for expats with partners who work away from home *(see Appendix 2)*.

A Successful Portable Business

"Have you heard of Tandem Nomads?" I ask a mum in the 'Solo Parenting Expat Mums' Facebook group. She is also fast becoming a friend.

"No, I haven't," she replies.

*"You **have to** join," I encourage her. "You will love it. You can totally work online with your training as a nutritionist. You could then have a business that would follow you wherever you move. You don't have to be at full capacity now, just join the group and start having a look at what*

others are doing. Look at what you can do now, even if it is just a few minutes a day."

"Really?" answers my friend, her face creasing into a smile on the screen in front of me. "This is so encouraging. I wasn't really thinking I could have a job because we keep moving all the time and I've got so much to do with the kids."

Amel Derragui is the founder of Tandem Nomads. She left a corporate career in marketing to follow love. She is passionate about entrepreneurship and helping people serve others. She is also adamant that accompanying expat spouses can have a career, aka a portable business, if they want to. The beauty of Amel's content is that you can do as little or as much as you can; from listening to her podcast on www.tandemnomads.com to finding a business idea through her Business Idea Accelerator or investing in her Portable Business Accelerator which has everything you need to guide you step-by-step to developing a fully-fledged online business. She adds: "Starting a business can be a very intimidating concept for some people, especially when solo parenting. But it does not have to be. Indeed, a portable business can be as small or big as you want. You can also start small and grow it when you have more time. A portable business provides you with the time and geographical flexibility you need as a solo parent. It also provides a track record and a resume that does not have holes when you are ready to get back to the labor market."

"Baby steps are the royal road to skill."
DANIEL COYLE

Chapter 3
One Couple

"I exist in two places, here and where you are."
MARGARET ATWOOD

Oxford, United Kingdom and Brazzaville, Congo, 2004
"Who is this girl who is writing to me?" Olivier wonders, curious, as he leans forward.

He reads the email again. The charity logo looks familiar.

Dear Olivier, the email reads, I am writing to you because one of my colleagues mentioned you may be able to proofread the resources that we produce in French. I am putting a team of volunteers together and was wondering if you would have time to help. I look forward to hearing from you. Warmly, Rhoda.

And so begins our conversation, or should I say, conversations.

We begin talking on the phone after Olivier calls me at the office to say hello and apologise for not being able to help with the proofreading. Our first phone conversation ends up lasting two hours (yes, on work time) but we are talking about how the organisation he works for trains its new staff. I have many questions since I am responsible for the induction of any new members joining the international team in our headquarters in Oxford. Olivier and I also have many friends in common and he even knows my boss!

He asks if he can call me at home.

We talk every evening that week. It is love at first conversation. He has travelled a lot and even knows the village in Lebanon where I was born. We share the same Christian faith and discovered early on that we attended the same youth conference some years back without knowing either of us was there! It feels like we have known each other for years.

He is on his way to another posting and would only have a short time in Switzerland. "We should meet up!" we conclude. How could we not?

It's the 31st of July 2004. I am flying into Geneva Airport so that we can meet. He is waiting for his passport to come back from work, so I am the one travelling. He doesn't know what I look like: he has disabled his email from reading attachments because his internet connection is so bad. I, on the other hand, have the advantage of having his photo: a handsome man kneeling by a waterfall, looking so rugged, he looks like a seasoned adventurer... Splendid, I had thought to myself when seeing it for the first time.

My plane is well over two hours late. As I come out at Arrivals, I scan the faces to see if he is there. My heart is racing. This is the first time we will lock eyes. What will he be like? Will we like each other?

"Olivier, is that you?" I ask a tall gentleman who seems to look like him.

"Yes, it is. Are you Rhoda?"

We have found each other in the crowd. Conversations are as fluid as ever as we talk about a recent trip I have taken to Lebanon.

Fast forward a year and a half, out of which we were in the same country for a combined total of four months, and we married in Switzerland on a beautiful winter's day. Our marriage was going to be a little different from the get-go. However, I was by no means prepared for the amount of travel he would be taking.

In the previous chapter, you will have checked-in on your own attitudes, feelings and needs. You cannot coerce or convince your partner to do anything in this chapter. If you have deep-rooted discord with your husband or wife, it may be better to reach out for couples' therapy with a relationship expert who understands the strains of global living.

Create a Joint Life

When asked in the 'Holding the Fort Abroad Survey' to choose the top five challenges of a couple's relationship due to work travel, 'staying friends' and 'emotional intimacy' came out top above 'reconnecting after a trip', 'parenting children' and 'agreeing on finances'. Yes, it could easily lead to living separate lives.

Up to now, our entire married life has included work travel for him. The first few years, he was doing one-to two-week trips. Although the twist was that he could get dispatched at any moment in case of a crisis.

One trip in 2008, which is forever etched in our memories, began with an emergency call asking Olivier to travel to Kenya where there was post-electoral violence. We were brand new parents and that trip deeply affected both of us.

He was seeing newborns, the same age as his son, in dire circumstances. I was a new mum in a country that was not my own.

He was in a war zone. I was in a country at peace.

He was seeing the effects of violence on ordinary people. I was crying myself to sleep because I was struggling to nurse the baby.

Neither of us could see what the other was living, nor truly understand the extent of the challenges faced. Not only were our geographical locations different, so were our experiences.

Over the years, he has frequently travelled to dangerous places. I remember once when he called on a satellite phone from a *wadi* (a valley that is dry except in the rainy season) in a war-torn country.

"Hello?" There is a question mark in my voice as I answer the phone from an unknown number. I don't normally answer those calls but I can't miss it in case it is him.

"Hello," a man's voice answers.

"Olivier?" I cry out. "Is that you? I thought you wouldn't be able to reach me at all during this trip?"

"I managed to find a satellite phone and I just wanted to hear your voice. I'm okay, everything is going well," he says reassuringly.

Relief floods my body, as I had been worried about his safety. But then I freeze, not knowing what to say. All I can think of is that this call is probably costing him a fortune and I don't want to waste the few minutes we have together telling him about the antics of the neighbours' cats, or some other unexciting titbit of my ordinary everyday life.

I find out later that he likes it when I share stories from my life. Not only does he crave a bit of normality, but it helps him to stay abreast of what is going on with me, even if my life may seem mundane.

"The family back home isn't living the only reality there is. I have my reality too from what I have lived," Olivier shared with me recently as we discussed the need to stay connected. Now when we tell the other what has been going on, we consolidate our stories to make one out of two.

We consolidate our stories to make one out of two.

Béatrice de Carpentier underscores the importance of telling each other about our everyday lives, because "it means sharing our respective realities and therefore builds up our life together".

One mother puts it this way: "It takes work to consolidate a joint life since this is made up of three realities: the absent spouse, the 'holding the fort' spouse and the joint reality of shared time together. For my husband and I, an important aspect of our joint life together is that wherever possible I have visited the places where he has been working; to share his experiences. This is something that we both value and have invested in. It has not always been possible; however, it is something we aspire to creating together. When it's not possible, I still want to be part of his reality in creating a joint life for us both. So I share photos, stories, all the mundane details of everyday life with colleagues, shopping, meeting local people. Whatever it is, I share as best I can.

"In holding the fort, he is able to come and go from my reality largely; perhaps my going away for a few days while he is home has enabled him to experience a deeper sense of my reality in terms of childcare, managing home life, and so on. This has helped us both, and for me to feel he 'gets it' – my reality. Both of us sharing in the deepest way possible feeds into our joint reality, our joint life, which of course is both home and away."

Béatrice also highlights the importance of the right 'heart attitude' for a couple to stay together. "Are you focusing on a life and a future together or have you let the possibility of separating as a couple creep into your thinking?" she asks. She has seen with her clients that often one partner presents the 'threat' of separation as a way of getting the other person's attention. This is actually expressing a cry to stay together. "This only plants a seed," she says, "that germinates and may end up leading the couple down a road they didn't want." She suggests that if the partner in fact wants to get closer to his or her partner, it is better never to mention separation but to find other ways to say it.

Another way of creating a joint life could be to work on a joint project that involves both of you, be it just a holiday away or a common passion. You can both be developing it, whether geographically apart or together. This provides continuity throughout the traveller's comings and goings.

One expat mum living in Thailand whose husband regularly travels for one to three weeks at a time writes: "Stay in contact – even if just by text or quick chat – to talk about the small daily stuff. Make space in the diary in the days before and after for time together. Make it non-negotiable."

Switching Rhythms

I have found over the years that I lead one kind of lifestyle when he is present and a very different one when he is absent. Rhythm and activities change.

Every time my husband is about to travel for work, I feel him withdrawing. I can tell that his mind is thinking ahead to the place he is going to, the job he needs to accomplish and how to start gathering what he needs. When he isn't travelling to the field for humanitarian work, then he is attending and presenting at conferences. Suitcases start piling up at the end of the bed, neat piles of papers beside them. Suitable outfits and equipment need to be sorted and I invariably help with fetching this or that.

Conversely, when he returns, if he has been gone longer than just a few days, it takes us a while to reconnect. As he re-enters the world of family and sharing life and space with a spouse, he has to change pace and readjust. I, too, as the spouse who has stayed at home, have to accept him back in and readjust to sharing the space with him.

"Oh my! Is that the time?" I look at the clock in the living room, feeling fully awake. After settling the children for bed, the house seems so quiet. It has been a welcome moment of peace. All the dishes are still piled up in the sink, but those can wait until the morning. "I am not about to use these precious moments of quiet for that," I mutter under my breath. But as usual, when Olivier is away, time runs away from me and I end up working late.

One Couple

There is also the time just after he has left, my sinking heart, and then I get into action mode.

One travelling husband in Canada puts it this way: "Get used to transition. The before and after is harder than the being away." He lists his challenges when returning home after a trip as 'feeling included back into the family', 'emotional intimacy' with his partner and 'loneliness'. Another dad acknowledges the challenge of both partners being tired when he returns from a trip. What is difficult, he writes, is "tiredness from travel, whilst my wife feels tiredness from solo parenting."

I laughed when I read Colleen's answer to the 'Holding the Fort Abroad Survey' question on whether there were acclimatisation times when her husband comes home after a trip. She writes: "He comes home energized to make life at home efficient. I am drained and feel like I've been in survival mode. Purging and revamping routines to be more efficient are not my top priority." When I interviewed her, she commented with a laugh that he is like a bulldozer, ready to deep clean all the cupboards and all she wants is to go out and eat in a nice restaurant. The last thing she wants is to deep clean. Sounds incredibly familiar. Either our husbands are surprisingly similar, or this is a common theme when travelling partners come home. This is what Mariam says about what happened when her husband used to come back from a business trip (they now both travel alternately): "I could handle the leaky roof. I could handle the burst water pipe, sickness with the kids, but the moment he came back and put the fork in the wrong kitchen drawer, that's when I would lose it. You definitely need time to get back to a new rhythm."

Robin Pascoe mentions in her book *A Moveable Marriage* that they had the '24-hour holding rule', meaning for that time, they have no expectations of each other. It gives each partner the chance to readjust to each other.

The Good Fight

Ever since our dating days, I have always been amazed at how an argument can break out even when we are thousands of miles apart. The conversation on the phone is going pleasantly enough; we are sharing what we have been up to, when, suddenly, one of us says something and an argument ensues. Thankfully (or not), these days we can read each other's expressions on camera, but arguing on the phone is difficult and making up even harder.

> *"Never go to bed mad. Stay up and fight."*
> **PHYLLIS DILLER**

According to Tara Parker-Pope, author of *For Better: How the Surprising Science of Happy Couples Can Help Your Marriage Succeed*, marriages need conflict. She writes: "The scientific study of marital conflict shows that couples need to rethink the role that conflict plays in their lives, and the opportunity it presents to improve their marriages. If you think about what you want from marriage – a soulmate, personal fulfilment, partnership – it makes sense that such ideals can be achieved only through a little negotiation, discussion, and argument." The trick is to know why we fight and how we fight (or long-distance fight, in our case). Keep reading as I unpack this...

Keep conflict situations healthy

Dr John Gottman and Dr Sybil Carrère led a six-year longitudinal study of 124 newlyweds. In 'Predicting Divorce among Newlyweds from the First Three Minutes of a Marital Conflict Discussion', published in *Family Process* in 1999, there are three crucial ways for ensuring conflicts are 'healthy', and these can be just as efficient when geographically apart.

Focusing on the first three minutes of an argument can change the whole tone of the conversation, according to their observations; they could even predict whether these couples, who had been married for less than nine months, were heading for divorce within six years. The couples were observed discussing a problem that was a source of ongoing disagreement in their marriage for about 15 minutes. In the couples who later divorce the study cites: "All started off their conflict discussions with significantly greater displays of negative emotion and fewer expressions of positive emotion when compared with couples who remained married over the course of the six-year study."

De-escalating an argument from afar is a challenge. Do you end the call? That would be an easy way to leave an argument in the middle and not pick it up until the next phone call! Maybe Phyllis Diller's quote should read: "Don't put the phone down, stay on the line and fight!" There may be circumstances outside our control which mean that we *have* to leave the conversation for a longer time than we normally would if we were having a face-to-face argument and this does make long-distance conflict more of a challenge. It is also harder to know under what circumstances each partner is coming to the discussion. But it might also be an advantage. Being forced to postpone the argument, and then not being physically in the same location, means there may be time for both parties to cool down and reflect. It may be that we both come back to the initial argument at a very different place than when we left it.

"When things are getting tense, when voices are rising and when tempers are flaring, do whatever it takes to calm it down," suggests Tara Parker-Pope. Sometimes just a simple statement like "I hate it when we fight" offers a break in the action and gives both sides an opportunity to ratchet down the conflict.

I have found that slowing down during a conflict can also help. Pause a moment before reacting; ask yourself what the real issue is. One argument could turn out to be about something much deeper.

"You and your spouse need to stick together no matter what," insists Karen, the mother living in Ireland, "even though you want to kill each other and you are miles apart. You might be on the phone telling him that your teenager is having a meltdown and he tells you that he needs to go to a concert with his work colleagues. You put the phone down and think, *If you were in front of me now, headlines tomorrow would be 'wife murders husband'.* In those times, remember what brought you together. There is light at the end of the tunnel, but work travel and expat life is not a situation for the fainthearted. It is something that requires nerves of steel, a toughness and resilience. No matter what, you have to keep going and you have to find tools that will assist you because it's so worth it at the end of the day."

Use the Distance

Living apart because of frequent business travel could actually present the ideal opportunity to work on your friendship. The trick is to use the distance to your advantage and adapt tools that are available. One travelling British husband living in New Zealand pointed out in the 'Holding the Fort Abroad Survey' that frequent business travel actually "gives you each time to reflect on the relationship."

Share an activity

We have always liked reading a book together. At the beginning of our marriage, one of us would read a chapter of our current book out loud to the other in bed. We spent many a happy evening curled up in this manner. It gave us common references and fostered togetherness. As children arrived and life took a more hectic turn, we abandoned this practice. This year has seen its revival in our relationship. We may not be able to read together in bed as much but each having our own copy, reading the same chapter and spending time discussing it online, has been a creative way to recreate the togetherness reading the same book brings us.

If you are not sure which activities to do, write a list separately first, then eliminate any that one of you won't enjoy and settle on those that you will both enjoy to some degree.

Andrea Schmitt is a Global Girl Coach. Her husband works in the hotel industry and travels at least three weeks every month. They have made it a habit to say good morning and goodnight every day. Our neighbours have breakfast with each other every morning on Skype.

Some ideas for long-distance activities could be to:

- Play an online game together.
- Watch a documentary at the same time.
- Take a walk outside while video-calling each other.
- Do some online shopping together.

Dates

"Make sure you have a weekly date night; it is absolutely vital that you spend time together to continue being friends," we were told in no uncertain terms at the beginning of our marriage.

We have failed miserably at being consistent with dates.

I mean, how on earth can we have a weekly date night if half the time we are on opposite sides of the planet? On top of that, every time we found a great babysitter, we moved. Or they moved.

Grandparents or siblings lived too far away to offer to take the children so we could have a weekend away. I remember the first time Olivier's parents took the children. We hadn't had proper time together in two years.

Does that mean our friendship is doomed and our marriage destined to fail?

Exciting date nights seem to be the answer. And those are totally doable when frequently apart. According to Tara Parker-Pope, couples don't need more "pleasant" activities – they need more exciting ones in order to hold on to the rush they felt when they first fell in love. So, don't despair if you don't manage to get as many dates as you would like.

Phone dates: four types of conversation

Over a coffee date one day, Olivier and I identified four different types of conversations we have on a regular basis. Identifying these has mostly helped to decide, when he is travelling, when we will have which conversation and at what frequency, depending on their level of priority.

1. Small interactions daily

These are essential, like saying good morning and goodnight, checking in to see if the other person is okay. Some couples need to touch base at least once a day, others can go a few days without.

2. Logistics conversations

These are unavoidable, but they could easily take over the bulk of your talking time. There are holiday dates and destinations to be determined, to-do lists of bills to pay and errands to run. We aren't always good at this, but when Olivier and I are able to list and discuss them in bulk rather than in a piecemeal fashion, it means that they aren't necessarily part of every conversation we have. You might want to schedule a specific time each week when you and your partner go over your planning and to-do lists.

3. Conversations about the children and taking parenting decisions together

These again could easily take over all of your conversations. Again, we try to list the topics and bring them up in bulk. Jotting down the decisions taken and potentially even the actions to be taken, like for the minutes of a business meeting, tends to be helpful!

4. The conversations about your relationship

Listed here last but by no means least important, are the conversations that touch on the dynamics between you, your needs as a couple and your level of intimacy. They tend to get pushed to the side as the busyness of life shouts louder. They will also be a place to share your dreams and goals and how you will support each other. Jennifer Petriglieri, author of *Couples That Work: How to Thrive in Love and at Work,* noticed during her research that most couples wanted to support each other but were not always clear on what they were supporting. She shares on episode 168 of the Tandem Nomads' Podcast *Dual career couples & putting the business at the same level as the partner's job* that sometimes partners think they are being supportive, when in fact, they are not giving the right type of support. By the way, evenings after you've both had a long day may not be the best time to have these chats. You may want to ensure you are both in a good headspace before embarking on them.

Conversations around these topics need to be put in the calendar intentionally. We have recently decided on a weekly phone date, wherever he is in the world, unless at home of course, that is exclusively dedicated to talking about our relationship and how we can strengthen it (unless there's an emergency, of course).

Identifying these different types of conversations and what proportion of time is dedicated to what topics ensures that not one type takes over above the others. It also means that we are able to pin down which conversations to have when he is back home.

Know your partner well

Dr Gottman has more advice for couples. His very first principle in his book *The Seven Principles for Making Marriage Work* is to make sure couples have an up-to-date love map of each other: "They remember the major events in each other's history, and they keep updating their information as the facts and feelings of their partner's world change... they know each other's life goals, hopes and dreams." This knowledge will strengthen the couple's relationship, which will in turn help them stay connected and weather together the storms of life. Keeping love maps updated is even more crucial if one or both partners travel for work.

Over the past few weeks, Olivier and I have asked each other the 60 questions in Dr Gottman's list such as: "Name one of your main rivals or enemies," or, "What is my dream getaway place?" These are questions we may once have known the answers to, but as our lives take on separate focuses and time is spent apart, the answers change and our partner may not know us in the present (and vice versa).

Keep the Romance Alive

This one is a very personal topic as so much depends on where each couple is at when it comes to intimacy and romance. What is certain though is that if you are harbouring negative feelings towards your partner, it will be hard to feel romantic towards them. The first thing I would say is that you can only work on yourself. Any work you can do on an individual level, whether it is greater awareness of your feelings, pursuing personal passions or projects, making time for reflection, will feed into your couple.

Some couples may find it easy to keep intimacy alive over the phone, others not so much. If that is the case, then focus on strengthening your friendship while apart, talk about your relationship if that is something feasible over the phone, swap emails or letters if that works for you. Think back to when you first met. Try going back to the way you communicated. And then, focus on the reconnecting times. The periods when your partner is back physically at home.

This is how Karen puts it: "You're a wife and a lover first and foremost. You have to maintain that passion, which is hard, because your husband is away all the time. He might come back and expect the passion to switch right back on, but we are thinking about the awful week we've just had, or what the children need. When he comes home, your husband wants you, just you, he wants your undivided attention. So do the kids. A mum's day stays the same every day. She is not on holiday when her partner comes home. But you have to give time to the romantic side of your relationship because it is important. On occasion, when we were able to get childcare, my husband and I actually booked ourselves into a hotel for the first night or two he was back so that we could connect again, chat and talk about the children."

I often feel stressed before my husband comes home. He gets offended because he thinks that I don't want him home. Not at all! It is just that when he is home, my attention feels divided, or to say it another way, it feels like double the attention is required to attend to kids and husband.

If you have had to deal with a crisis alone while your partner was gone, your first feeling when they return may be anger. Taking those hours away gives you space to straighten situations out before your partner comes home and gets sucked into repairs, household chores and children demanding their attention.

Some couples will be able to reconnect straight away when the traveller returns. One mother mentioned to me how easily she and her partner reconnect on the surface but then the real work of reconnection begins over the first few days as the traveller settles back into the family life and routine, figuring out what has changed and what has stayed the same while they were gone.

And let's remember to try and include some fun. "Every couple needs some novelty," confirms Béatrice de Carpentier. "Bringing playfulness into our relationship as a couple can help."

Finding something fun to do together despite the distance and when we are home together is the key. My husband discovered Q Cards (www.qcards.co.uk) not long ago and suggested we use them for dates. These question cards are sorted into three types: *Reflect* (designed as conversation starters), *Reveal* (bringing out deeper replies), *Relate* (these questions elicit answers specific to your couple). As each deck is placed face down, conversation starts by taking it in turns to answer *Reflect* questions. When you are both ready, move on to the *Reveal* and *Relate* piles. "Which, of all our dates, would you go back and experience again?" is one such question or "What stands out as your favourite birthday memory?"

Two Travellers

*"In an ideal marriage, we do not merge
but maintain our separateness and differing ideas."*
PHYLLIS ADLER

Everyone will have their own expectations of what an ideal marriage is. You may or may not agree with the quote above – I'm not even sure a marriage is ideal all the time. What I have seen though, as I have interviewed and observed couples, is that there are seasons. You may have been at home for years, creating a home, raising children and moving from one country to the next, but if you want, there is a way of working outside the home, it may just not be what you had pictured.

It won't be easy. Schedules may need more juggling, but you don't need to work 100% in one go. Others may judge or not understand. Mariam Ottimofiore shares how bothered she is by society's perception of her husband's absence: "When my husband is traveling and I'm at home, nobody asks me how I am doing or if I need help because the expectation is that I should be able to manage everything. But when I'm gone, he gets so many invitations and offers to drop off meals!

There are so many double standards and we're trying to actively fight against these. Men traveling is seen as the norm and nobody checks up on the wife. When the wife travels, everyone's asking me if I've frozen meals for him for while I'm gone."

Jennifer Petriglieri's book *Couples That Work: How to Thrive in Love and at Work* can help here. She goes beyond the practical ways of balancing two careers and delves into motivations and expectations that come into play when both partners work. She points out that couples go through three major transitions: making two independent lives work together, what the couple and each partner really wants (born out of frustrations and inner questioning) and then a redefinition of roles, identities and goals as couples become empty nesters or are seen as the older generation. Being aware of these transitions could be key while navigating being a couple, and why not, a dual-career couple, even if the timeline is longer than you would like.

Cultural Clashes

"If we are going to live with our deepest differences then we must learn about one another."
DEBORAH J LEVINE

You may wonder what being in an intercultural relationship has to do with a spouse frequently travelling for work. Well, if partners come from two different cultures, this has the potential for some misunderstandings that can lead to serious relationship trouble. You have enough to deal with from living abroad and being alone a lot. Increasing the quality of your communication will benefit your relationship.

Culture is everywhere around us. It is in what people believe, how they behave, what they assume, how they 'do' life, what is important to them. When there are patterns in these areas that go beyond personality and individual differences, culture emerges. Most people are already part of various cultures (musical, generational, professional, for example). Two people starting a family unit will bring with them a whole set of values and ways of seeing the world that they have subconsciously learned from the environment they were raised in.

While on the surface cultural differences might be obvious, like the way we greet each other or the foods that we eat, there are a lot of components that go into relationships, like how we give and receive negative feedback, whether it is rude to question authority, whether our meaning is crystal clear or buried under layers of 'code', to name but a few examples.

According to Expat Insider 2018, "Among expats in a relationship, only 43% have a partner with the same nationality, 35% are involved with a national of the host country and 22% with someone from yet another country." That's a combined 57% who are in a relationship with a partner from a different country. I'd say these figures demonstrate that it is important to look at cultural differences closely, not only as we move geographically from one country to another but also as we live multiculturally in our own families.

You may feel like a cultural chameleon, able to blend into any communication style and culture, but not everyone is highly-attuned to this.

"Oh, I don't need to talk about culture, because I get along with a lot of people from many cultures," people say to me.

"Until you have a conflict with someone and can't figure out why," I reply with my tongue slightly in my cheek.

If you keep hitting a wall in a relationship, it might be worth double-checking cultural differences in communication. These may be so subconscious that it wouldn't occur to you or your partner that the conflict you keep experiencing over and over again can be resolved through a better understanding of a cultural aspect in your life.

> You may feel like a cultural chameleon, able to blend into any communication style and culture, but if you keep hitting a wall in a relationship, it might be worth double-checking cultural differences in communication.

For example, I would get upset when my husband 'criticised' something I had done. I would take it personally and question our relationship. If he shot down my work, I would imagine he thought I was a failure. As I learnt about different ways of giving negative feedback, everything took on another perspective. I understand now that he was not attacking my worth as a person but only giving direct feedback to my work, which is totally acceptable in his culture.

Overseas assignments, the stress of coping with travelling partners and adapting to a new culture can bring the couple to polarising behaviour. "Individual differences become more pronounced, conflict is more entrenched, and there is a general lack of tolerance toward each other," explains Yvonne McNulty in 'Till stress do us part: the causes and consequences of expatriate divorce' published in the *Journal of Global Mobility: The Home of Expatriate Management Research* in 2015.

"When dealing with life's problems, we tend to go back to our roots, which gives us a sense of comfort and identity. But the ways we choose may be perplexing to our partners."
DUGAN ROMANO

It is also a question of cultural values. The more you know yourself and your cultural influences, the faster you will bridge the gap between you and your partner. It is just as important to know the way you communicate as to know your personality style, values and beliefs.

Views regarding gender roles can differ a lot from one person to another. Differences in culture do not necessarily stem from growing up in two different countries either. Family cultures, faith cultures, socio-economic backgrounds bring with them sets of values and expected behaviours, so much so that two individuals from the same country may find themselves diametrically opposites in terms of gender roles, to keep that example. The pressure for the wife to leave paid work and 'only' manage the home and family may get stronger if her husband is away. For others, on the contrary, mothers are encouraged to have a career and children put in day care, which in some countries is hardly ever questioned.

Mary is French and married to James, an American. They both live in Switzerland, where they met. Their first child was born a year ago. She has been offered a senior position in the Human Resources department of a French company. She knows that her husband will be travelling a lot for his work and that she is going to have to juggle a lot but in France, where she grew up, many children go to the crèche as babies. It's what everybody does. Where James grew up, mothers stay at home and look after the children. Mary has a dilemma and their respective families don't seem to understand the different perspectives.

What you are looking out for

The encouraging element of culture is that there is a framework to it. It is not random. There are ways to understand the origin of unexplained clashes. Many sociologists have categorised these elements.

Understanding how different cultures communicate can lead to many 'lightbulb' moments and soothe many fraught relationships. This is especially poignant if the disagreement occurs during a phone conversation you are having with your husband, who is miles away in another country, and you are left with the unpleasant after-taste of an unresolved argument after putting the phone down.

Understanding how different cultures communicate can lead to many 'lightbulb' moments and soothe many fraught relationships.

In this book I cannot go into all the cross-cultural elements but let me share with you those that I have found have impacted my relationship with my husband in the context of him travelling and us communicating over the phone (see *Resources* for further reading on cross-cultural relationships).

The Lewis Model was articulated by Richard Lewis in his book *When Cultures Collide* (1996). The study is based on data drawn from 50,000 executives taking residential courses and more than 150,000 online questionnaires to 68 different nationalities. Lewis concluded that humans can be divided into three clear categories based on behaviour: Linear-active, Multi-active and Reactive.

While the three types are separate, each possesses behavioural elements from the other two categories. It is a question of which behaviours are dominant.

Here are a few of the characteristics relating to communication in each of Lewis' three categories:

Linear-actives: Talks half the time. Polite but direct. Rarely interrupts. Truth before diplomacy.

Multi-actives: Talks most of the time. Displays emotions. Often interrupts. Flexible truth.

Reactives: Listens most of the time. Polite. Conceals feelings. Doesn't interrupt.

Richard Harris attributes each category to a side of a triangle. You can access it on the Cross Culture website (www.crossculture.com).

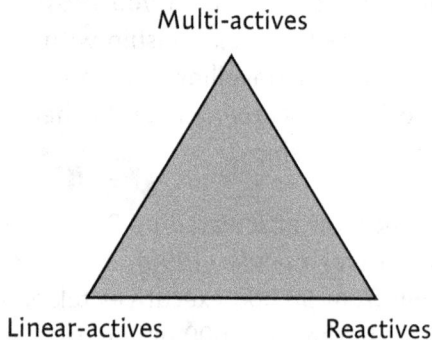

Multi-actives

Linear-actives   Reactives

My Triangle:

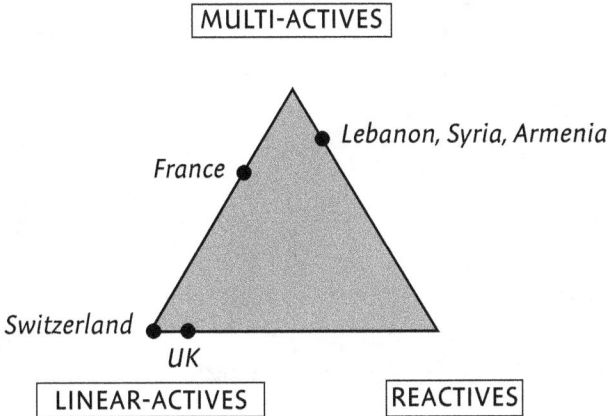

"So, I'm not that weird!"

Imagine a Multi-active speaking on the phone to their partner (a Linear) while on a work trip. The former continuously speaking and wondering why their partner doesn't jump in with comments, while the latter stays silent and waits for an opportunity to speak that never comes. Right here is a source of cultural misunderstanding that can easily be remedied and help avoid needless conflict and resentment.

My siblings and I grew up with a culture from each side of the pyramid. Our behaviours, those of our parents and our life partners suddenly start making a lot more sense.

Write down the different countries you have lived in yourself (France, England, for example), second, where your parents are from (in my case Syria and Wales) and third, where your partner is from and then visualise where they would be on the triangle. You may realise why sometimes your life seems erratic and/or in the words of my dear sister exclaim: "So, I'm not that weird!"

Pauses

It is all the more important to pay attention to these as conversations are held over the phone. Even with a screen, where we can see each other's face, signs may be missed.

I must admit that in the early years of our marriage, I wasn't even aware that my husband put pauses in his conversation. I would just speak incessantly and not really listen to what he said or didn't say! I have since learnt that really listening to what someone says means listening not only to the words they choose but also to what they repeat, how they say things and what they don't say! This is especially important if most of our interactions with our significant other are on the phone.

I have also learned to respect my husband's pauses. To be exact, I am still learning that and counting to myself helps. Try it. Count to 10 (or more) when they stop speaking to see if they start again.

Pauses during conversations can be due to personality differences. And this is where it is important to know your personality and your partner's personality. Susan Storm is a certified Myers-Briggs Type Indicator practitioner. You can find out more about this and even do a personality test on www.mbtionline.com. In her article 'How to Spot Each Myers-Briggs® Personality Type in Conversation', she explains that some personality types take regular pauses during conversation – to consider the impact their words are having on their interlocutor, to think because their thought process is internal, or to find just the right word.

Kristina Lundholm Fors' academic thesis 'Production and Perception of Pauses in Speech', published on *Semantic Scholar* in 2015, identifies that a typical pause in speech lasts only about a quarter to half a second. A long pause (approximately four seconds) can seem like a long time and make the conversation awkward. This shows that a few seconds' difference in a pause can still be perceived and interpreted.

'Talk is Silver, Silence is Golden: A Cross-Cultural Study on the Usage of Pauses in Speech', a joint study by the University of Augsburg and the Tokyo University of Agriculture and Technology, published on *ResearchGate* in 2008, took into account pauses that lasted for more than one second, then those that lasted for over two seconds in the German and Japanese cultures. They found out that Japanese subjects used significantly more pauses at both lengths than German subjects.

They quote Geert Hofstede's individualism and collectivism dimension: "On the individualist side ties between individuals are loose, and people are expected to take care for themselves. On the collectivist side, people are integrated into strong, cohesive in-groups, often extended families which continue protecting them in exchange for unquestioning loyalty. Germany lies on the individualistic side of this dimension, whereas Japan is a collectivistic culture. He states that in collectivistic cultures silence may occur in conversations without creating tension." This difference could also be because high-context languages also use more pauses.

Saying what you mean, or not

This section is going to look at what is called high and low context cultures. Essentially, the terms low and high-context cultures explain that low-context cultures say what they mean and mean what they say, while for others (the high-context ones), you read between the lines according to the context. The concept of high and low context was introduced by anthropologist Edward T Hall in his 1976 book *Beyond Culture*.

I'll give you an example from my own life. Olivier and I were taking my mother out shopping. Bear in mind she's Syrian-Armenian, lived in France for forty years, is married to a Welshman and currently lives in England. In this story, I would say she was communicating from a high-context.

"I can't find the plant that I was looking for," Mum *complains as she and I walk around the garden centre. She has been wanting to buy this particular plant for a long time.*

One Couple

"Shall we go to a bigger garden centre?" I ask, eager for her to find the plant she wants. "Olivier and I don't mind taking you, even if it is a longer drive."

"Well, don't bother, let's go home," she says, hesitantly.

Here we go, *I think*, she says she wants to go home but it sounds like she wants to go to the bigger garden centre.

"We can drive you if you want."

"No," she replies, again hesitantly. "Don't bother."

We just can't figure out what she wants to do. It really sounds like she wants to go. Why is she saying she doesn't? Or is she?

In general, anthropologists classify Anglo, Nordic and Germanic cultures as 'low-context'; Latin-European, Latin American, Arabic and Far Eastern cultures are classified as 'high-context'.

Erin Meyer, in her book *The Culture Map*, points out that there is the most potential for misunderstandings between two high-context communications than any other combination. She also warns about relative places on the scale – as one may seem higher context than another even if they are both on the low end.

> There is the most potential for misunderstandings between two high-context communications.

She further highlights eight different cultural scales (communicating in high/low contexts, giving negative feedback, persuasion by giving principles first or examples of applications, hierarchical or egalitarian leading, top-down or consensual decision-taking, trusting, disagreement and time). She shows how some cultures can be close on some aspects and quite different on others. She warns against making assumptions about individuals based on where they are from but insists on the usefulness of being aware of cultural differences.

She explains how countries were placed: mid-level managers were interviewed and asked what would be considered appropriate business behaviour on these different topics. She explains: "a normative pattern emerges. A bell curve illustrates the range of what is considered appropriate [...] the country position on the scale indicates the mid position of a range of acceptable and appropriate behaviours in that country." *The Culture Map* is written with business teams in mind but is oh-so-useful if you are an intercultural family.

One country doesn't necessarily equal one culture. The *Harvard Business Review* article 'Research: The Biggest Culture Gaps Are Within Countries, Not Between Them' summarises the study by Bradley Kirkman, Vas Taras and Piers Steel published in *Management International Review* in May 2016. The study actually highlights that "country is actually a very poor 'container' of culture." It is just as important to look at patterns of communication and behaviours that are learnt in childhood, through educators, and through the communities we have learnt them from. If you would like to take this further, Csaba Toth, the founder of ICQ Global, has developed the Global DISC, an "ICF accredited, multi-award-winning behavioural model" which combines personality type and cultural background.

A New Equilibrium

In her article entitled 'Please, Don't Call Me a Trailing Spouse' in *Global Living Magazine* in April 2015, Claire Bolden McGill acknowledges that there is often "little equilibrium in the relationship at the start" and "when each of you experiences new events and moments separately, you can begin to feel jealous or resentful." She offers hope though: "Once you've gone beyond that and found your balance, learn to live your own lives, and share joined-up lives, things begin to work out."

I do love that accompanying spouses are now called STARS: Spouses Travelling and Relocating (and often solo parenting, I might add) Successfully. This term was coined in around 2007 by Apple Gidley, author of *Expat Life: Slice by Slice*.

Chapter 4
When Storms Come

"A story to me means a plot where there is some surprise. Because that is how life is – full of surprises."
ISAAC BASHEVIS SINGER

Nyon, Switzerland, 2008
I open my eyes and look around the room. Light is shining through the blinds and I can hear birds chirping in the yard outside. But something is off; a strange white fog is covering everything.

"Olivier," I whisper, as I turn to see if he is awake. "I'm scared, my eyes have gone all funny."

"What? What do you mean?" he replies. He's still feverish, I can tell. Since coming home from his last trip a week ago he has been lying in bed with a 40°C temperature, unable to get up except to drag himself to the bathroom. The doctors are still trying to figure out what has made him so sick.

"Everything is in a heavy white mist and it's not going away. I can hardly see my hand when it is in front of my face."

"Oh gosh, Rhoda, you need to get to an ophthalmologist, quick."

The local ophthalmologist's equipment is not strong enough to diagnose the problem, so she refers me to the corneal specialist at the world-renowned Hôpital Ophtalmique Jules Gonin in Lausanne.

"You will probably see an assistant, not the specialist," she warns. *"It is August and all the hospitals have slowed down for the summer. In addition, people come from all over Europe to this clinic so there will be a waiting period."*

I get an appointment for the following week.

"Excuse me a minute," says the assistant, after spending 20 minutes examining my eyes. *"I need to ask the specialist to come and check something."*

I am worried now. What is going on?

A few minutes later, in walks a tall, handsome man in his thirties. His stride is confident, his face relaxed, with not a hint of strain. Just as well, I think as I smile to myself remembering a comment my father-in-law once said about doctors and nurses getting younger the older he gets.

His greeting is friendly and he speaks in a soft voice.

"Has anyone ever mentioned the word 'keratoplasty' to you before?" he asks.

"No," I reply.

"You are going to need a corneal transplant in each eye,"
he explains.

I start crying as I tell him that my husband is ill, we have
a nine-month-old and I don't have family around.

It is one thing to manage a life abroad and a fly-in, fly-
out partner when life is going at a relatively manageable
pace. But some situations become extreme due to
sickness, death or mental health struggles and these
needs put a greater strain on the relationship and the
individual.

"Don't take drastic action if exceptional circumstances
strain your couple and bring difficulties between you,"
cautions Béatrice de Carpentier. "These difficulties,
although real, are exacerbated and may not reflect you
as a couple in 'normal' circumstances. Wait until things
calm down."

Stephen Covey writes in *The 7 Habits of Highly Effective
People* of the moment that changed his life. He was
perusing books in a library when he came across this
statement: "Between stimulus and response, there is a
space. In that space is our power to choose our response.
In our response lies our growth and our freedom."

It is also a useful principle when responding to a crisis.
Pause, just pause, even for a fraction of a second.
Remember in that time to include yourself in the
response-scenario.

Illness

Chronic illness is not planned, it never is. "It can be extremely stressful when we, or someone we love, becomes ill abroad. As well as the (very normal) physical and mental turmoil of illness, we often find ourselves dealing with additional challenges that are unique to international life," writes Carolyn Parse Rizzo in her article 'The Challenges and Opportunities in Managing a Health Condition Abroad', published online for *Families in Global Transition* (FIGT) in March 2019. Carolyn is a Certified Child Life Specialist and Life Coach for Global Families. Along with Health Psychologist Vivian Chiona, Founder and Director of Expat Nest, she led a Kitchen Table discussion around this topic at the FIGT conference. Their collaboration highlights eight challenges:

1. Lack of information of local health system.
2. Potential for a difficult financial situation.
3. Feeling isolated.
4. Being overwhelmed.
5. Possible mistrust.
6. Possible miscommunication.
7. 'Complex parenting' (where one parent may need to be at the hospital and picking up kids from school at the same time because there is no one else).
8. Pain and discomfort.

If your partner is away on a trip, this can be particularly difficult, notwithstanding dealing with the illness or incident itself. Creating a 'healing team' around you is one of the strategies Carolyn and Vivian highlight from their talks with participants. Being proactive about finding out about the healthcare system is another. This can certainly be done together, in partnership with your partner, or one of you can take the lead in finding out the basics of how it works. Being aware of the extra challenges you will be facing and harnessing the strategies Vivian and Carolyn offer is a great help if illness abroad is something you are facing. You can read more tips on Vivian's blogpost '16 Strategies to manage a health condition abroad' published on the Expat Nest website in April 2018.

Ageing Parents

"To care for those who once cared for us is one of the highest honors."
TIA WALKER

"We will need to keep an eye on my parents," says Olivier to me as he is about to board a plane for his next business trip.

"*I* will need to keep an eye on **your** parents, you mean," I reply, smiling, gently correcting his assumption that we would both be taking care of them.

As we discuss his parents' declining health and what we need to watch out for, I realise that he is right: we need to do this together. Being miles away from his parents doesn't mean that he can't make sure they are well and that we can't work as a team on this. We agree there and then that:

- I will visit my parents-in-law every two weeks with the boys.
- He will call them once a week to talk. He will tell me if he felt there was something that I needed to follow up on.

As it turns out, he called his parents one Sunday morning only to be passed to a neighbour who told him the situation was bad and we needed to intervene immediately. My mother-in-law had weakened so much in the few weeks since I had last seen her that she needed help at home, my father-in-law having not been able to help for years.

As I also help my own mother from far away, I am learning that there are plenty of things you can do to help an ageing parent even from abroad: play online games, sit by the phone while they fall asleep (I got all teary-eyed in *that* role reversal), call during the hardest part of their days, order any special items or food they need and so much more. My mum was having trouble falling asleep. As I know that she grew up by the sea, I bought her a noise machine so she could listen to the waves. She loves it so much she bought herself another one so she can listen downstairs too!

Caring for an ageing parent from abroad is about listening to what they say and thinking outside the box as to how you can help fill any need they mention. It is also about asking questions, delving a bit deeper into a problem they are explaining.

The conversations you or your partner have with ageing parents who live long-distance can be a true lifesaver for them and have a lasting positive effect as well as alleviate the load for a sibling who is caring for them on a more day-to-day, practical level. The emotional aspect of caring for them is just as meaningful as the practical one and this is a space that you can occupy, even from abroad. *Parental Guidance, Long Distance Care for Aging Parents* by Ana McGinley has a lot of sound advice and tips, especially around distance and dementia, and other illnesses around ageing. She writes: "Distance should not stop you being able to participate in conversations about future plans for your parent. As a close family member, you have the right, some people would argue responsibility, to be part of the process." She reminds us that we have a long history of knowing our parents and are therefore well equipped to be their advocate.

Caring for a parent from abroad at the same time as your partner is away for work is going to draw on your time, your physical energy and your emotional bank. This is a time to be extra aware of where you spend your time, how much rest and relaxation you are getting, what and who replenishes you.

Losing a Loved One

My father passes away in the night, on Sunday the 30th

of September 2019. I always thought I would be able to rush to his bedside, if necessary. We are only an hour and a half plane ride away. I hadn't anticipated that he would have an internal haemorrhage in the middle of the night and slip away within a few hours.

The children are in bed. Olivier has been away for five weeks for work. He is due back on Tuesday. I sit on the bottom step of the staircase leading up to our second floor, cuddling my knees and rocking gently to and fro. The cats sitting at my feet sense something is wrong and rub against my leg. "What an amazing comfort these cats have turned out to be," I murmur through my tears. In a way, I'm not alone. The phone buzzes and beeps the whole night as my brother, sister and I communicate across three countries.

The next day, I grit my teeth and fly to England with our two boys. After three flights and over 7,000 km travelled, Olivier joins us in England, exhausted.

Those days were tough. I was grieving, big time, and didn't give Olivier space to re-enter the family sphere. We discussed this time many months later and re-emphasised the need to extend each other grace when extra challenges put pressure on us individually and as a couple.

Dangerous Situations

What about times when one member or more of the

family finds themselves in fragile contexts? Many partners travel for humanitarian purposes or for the foreign service on behalf of their government. This adds another layer of complexity to the travel and the separation.

Splitting a family for an evacuation

Founder of Expats on Purpose and host of the podcast *Expat Happy Hour*, Sundae Schneider-Bean had to take some tough decisions in January 2016. At the time, she and her family were living in Burkina Faso. After a terrorist attack particularly close to home, Sundae and her husband decided to split the family. "It was one of those things," she explains. "Even though we didn't want to go, it felt like it was the best choice for our family, for me to go with the boys and my husband stay back and finish his assignment. Within 10 days, we made an abrupt transition to Switzerland. I was running my company full-time and solo parenting my boys while he was finishing his assignment." Sundae and her husband had discussed in advance what would trigger an evacuation for them even if her husband's organisation didn't mandate it. If it was important to them, then they would take all steps necessary. "The criteria that we had laid out objectively had well been exceeded by that terrorist attack. I didn't want to go, I didn't want to rip my family apart. I didn't want to leave the country I loved. But it was one of those things where we had a huge wake up call. I always tell my clients, instead of thinking about staying or going as a strategic decision, think about what your values are."

Instead of thinking about staying or going as a strategic decision, think about what your values are.

Her advice? Take decisions that will align with your values even if it may seem like you are 'less brave' than other expats if you decide to fly back to your home country in a dangerous situation. Understand the parameters from your sending organisation, and plan in advance for the unexpected. This way you can be prepared to potentially self-finance if a departure is not funded by the organisation. After taking their decision, Sundae and her husband trusted that they had the skills to make it work. "I also reached out to two seasoned expat women I knew had experienced long-distance relationships. I wanted to reduce my uncertainties and know the challenges I could be facing."

Dangerous jobs

When Olivier was doing humanitarian field work, we would often host dinners where a dozen or so seasoned humanitarian workers would share stories of their times in various countries.

Some stories were funny as they recounted their silly blunders in an overseas location. A vegetarian in the group recalled how once she had purposefully arrived late at a festive meal she had been invited to so that she wouldn't have to decline eating meat, only to find that they had waited for her! Other stories were harrowing. I remember the time they reminisced about being heliported on the top of a mountain and having to hike the rest of the way in the freezing cold with heavy supplies of blankets and food in order to help inmates in a prison, or, in war-torn countries, when mothers pleaded with them to take their children and tried to physically force them into the car as the time came for the humanitarian workers to leave.

It amazes me that Olivier and his team were never debriefed by a Mental Health Professional on their return from difficult trips, or at the very least offered the opportunity to speak to one. If they were having trouble processing the violence and inhumanity they were experiencing, it seems they would 'offload' amongst themselves. It was naturally often difficult for Olivier to adjust on his return from these kinds of trips. He would often be silent, withdrawn, sad and wouldn't necessarily want to burden me with his stories. When he did open up sometimes, I had to stop him as I just couldn't handle the trauma he would recount seeing. He would hold his children that much closer to tell them how much he loved them. There were so many stories he wasn't allowed to tell or couldn't bring himself to. The humanitarians and those working in difficult, war-torn countries carry a heavy burden and have earned my utmost respect.

The article 'Being Married to Someone with a Dangerous Job' by Julia Austin on www.madamenoire.com in September 2018 is a rare admission of common feelings when married with someone who puts their life on the line for their job: "We desperately want them to quit their job, and simultaneously would never ask them to because it is part of who they are, and the 'world needs them.'" Let us not discount the challenges though. Have you ever been on the phone with them, describing a crisis at home and they are interrupted by a 'work' crisis they absolutely must deal with? It is worth having a conversation with your partner about 'emergencies'. Share with them your concerns when they 'have to run off' somewhere. Figure out together if you can minimise hurting each other during those times.

Mental Health

It is uncanny. As I write this section, my father-in-law has tested positive for Covid-19 and is in hospital. My mother-in-law is in her final days of life in palliative care. I will be tested today as I have a sore throat. Hubby is in transit on a plane. We will wait for the results of my test before we know if he can come home. As I wake up at 3.30 am and pace the living room, my teeth start to chatter, my body to shiver. Thankfully, there is a number to call, 143 – La Main Tendue in Switzerland, to speak to someone anonymously and confidentially. The service is available 24/7 and free.

"Take it one step at a time," she reminds me.

"I'm scared," I answer.

"I hear you. What exactly are you afraid of?" she asks.

As I speak to the lovely lady on the other side of the line and hear her soothing voice, my nerves start to settle.

Sometimes it is hard to notice when our mental health is declining. We are so engrossed in 'keeping our heads above water' that we may not realise we are dealing with inner turmoil. With pressure from outside turning into strain within, we must juggle a million things, a weight on our chest. No one to talk to when your partner isn't home. Except that even if they were home, or available to talk every time you need them, it may not be enough. You may need more professional help. Someone who has experience of what you are going through and why.

Karen readily recalls how precious it was to reach out to a Psychologist when she needed help dealing with the stresses of her husband's frequent travels and the unique challenges their children had, that she could not handle alone. She readily admits though that if she hadn't had a dear friend who was a mental health professional, she probably wouldn't have sought counsel and would have missed out on the expert help that person offered her.

"Talking about your experience can be a challenge at times, but it's worth it. By being vocal, you can develop more coping skills, stronger relationships and a stronger sense of self," reads the first tip on the *Be Vocal Speak Up* website. You can find a professional to speak to in the International Therapist Directory or in a more immediate crisis there is a list of helplines from around the world in *Resources*.

Chapter 5
Parenting Together

"As a parent, you are more important than you know."
KATHLENE SENEY-WILLIAMS

Bern, Switzerland, 2019
"Mummy, could I have a mobile phone, please? Everyone in my class has one," our 13-year-old asks, flapping his eyelids at me and joining his hands together in prayer.

I sigh. This is a conversation that I have been putting off for as long as possible. He has already asked me on multiple occasions, but I kept telling him we'd talk another day. I really feel I owe him a clear decision. But it is such a big one! Once children have a smartphone, it is so much harder to backtrack and take it off them. On the other hand, kids these days have them earlier and earlier. It would be nice for him to have a phone to call me if necessary when he is with his friends.

"I promise you I will look into it," I reply, "and we will come up with a proper contract between us," I say, as I start debating with myself the pros and cons of a phone, what restrictions should be set on it and when on earth I will find the time to figure it all out.

And then it strikes me; this is a parenting conversation to have with Olivier. This is an opportunity to parent together. As he and I discuss over the phone, there is a connection between us that even the miles can't squash.

Parenting Together

It is not just the conversations **about** the children to have with the travelling parent, it is the parenting decisions that need to be **taken**; some can be decided even if both parents are miles away from each other.

A friend of mine recently made a comment that I was a single parent. I'm not.

Single parenting is when a person is a parent and is single – because their partner has left altogether, has sadly passed away or the couple is separated or divorced. The other parent may or may not be in their children's life.

When a person is a parent and is married/in a committed relationship, and the other parent is away for work or living in another location for some reason, that is solo parenting. The day-to-day of parenting rests on the non-travelling parent's shoulders but the whole of parenting shouldn't. Just as it is a challenge to stay a couple in long-distance relationships, so it is a challenge to parent together when one is away a lot for work.

Dawn Purver is a Psychotherapist who knows first-hand what it is like to live, work and raise children overseas, including what it means to have a travelling partner. "The responsibility lies with the travelling parent to be involved in the children's lives and know what is going on," she says in response to whether having a travelling parent is detrimental to the children. "It comes down to the quality of the communication." She encourages a long-distance parent to think about what they could do to make each of their children feel loved. Family members may feel that there is loss involved around the parent's physical absence and it is important to acknowledge it but there are also great gains. Their absence may make their presence on their return so much more precious and the times spent together more meaningful. Weekends away with just one child can be a good way of deepening the bond between parent and child and is worth the extra intention and planning.

One mother echoes this in the 'Holding the Fort Abroad Survey'. She writes: "In terms of parenting, I feel we have been able to use this situation in some good ways. As the stay at home parent, I have made sure my son and I have special activities when my husband is away – we may go to the movies, or watch TV shows we both like, or I take him out to dinner, or eat fun food at home. For my son and I, this has given special bonding times for us that will always be special mother and son times. Then when my husband comes home, we try to make sure they go and do special father and son activities (and I get some time to myself) as well as family times together. Frequent work travel has made us more intentional with the 'bonding' time we spend with our son."

Frequent work travel has made us more
intentional with the 'bonding'
time we spend with our son.

That is the challenge: for the parent who is not physically present to be present and involved in parenting decisions. How can they be hands-on even if they are miles away?

Involving the parent who is not physically present needs to have a two-pronged approach. It is important for the parent who is away to try different approaches to make their presence felt. It is also up to the other parent and the extended family to help keep them a full member of the family.

One great resource, if you are able to, is to turn to a Parenting Coach. Sharoya Ham is founder of Embracing Behavior Change. Being on the same screen as my husband, around the topic of parenting our children and being asked what we each want most for our kids, was extremely powerful and symbolic of our togetherness in parenting. Although three time zones apart, over one screen, Sharoya prompted us to think about what parenting means for us, what behaviours we want to see our children display and what visions we have for our relationship with them.

The Travelling Parent

The US National Public Radio interviewed three parents who were living apart from their children.

Owen Kibenge was one of them. He is a freelance journalist from Uganda and dad of one. He was away from his son while he attended graduate school in the USA. Interestingly, when he returned home, his wife took a turn at studying abroad and he stayed home with their son. He shares that the parent living away must be careful not to get offended if the children don't ask to speak to them on the phone. The child may not be saying "I want Daddy" or "I want Mummy", but it is important to "insert yourself and find creative ways to stay engaged". He finds that often when a conversation gets to the fact that he has a child and that he is long-distance, it is dismissed, as if it is normal. "It's almost as if because I am the father and I am the one who is away, they're implicitly saying that it's okay. In my head, I'm like, no, no, it's not okay – I'm not cool with it at all."

Insert yourself and find creative ways to stay engaged.

It is one thing to want to be involved from miles away, it is quite another to make it happen.

Dan Verdick's book, *The Business Traveling Parent: How to Stay Close to Your Kids When You're Far Away*, is a collection of over 100 creative and fun ideas that will help before, during and after a trip. At one point, he does mention tape recorders, but all his suggestions are timeless. He suggests, for example, creating a keepsake box where your child can keep all the art and school projects they'll want to show you when you get back or a secret code that you can use to write emails and letters. He writes: "Focus on process, not product. The activity doesn't need to be perfect – you just want to have fun together."

A friend of mine pointed me to www.hugahero.com, a site where you can buy a doll with a photo of Mummy or Daddy on it! You can even have a voice message recorded and placed inside the doll. Started by two wives of US Marines, they soon realised that other professions called parents away from their children. They share that kids hug their dolls at the doctor's for extra comfort or take it shopping and on other outings.

Stay engaged

For fathers or mothers who want to stay engaged with their children, even when living away, there is a lot to be learned from divorced mums and dads who share custody of their child. Some of these parents live not too far away geographically but will only see their children intermittently. The resources available for them can give travelling parents some useful advice. George Newman's *101 Ways to be a Long-Distance Super Dad or Mom, Too!* is written to help parents not living under the same roof as their kids "build and maintain good, strong relationships with their children." It has been adopted by family court systems and distributed by military chaplains to members of the armed services. Not all his 101 suggestions will suit a family where both parents are still married, yet living in different locations, but many will. He suggests, for example, making a scrapbook of childhood memories, photos of you as a child, places you visited, things you did. Your child may be surprised by what you did and they will get to know you better. This may compensate for the stories you are not able to tell 'off the cuff' if you were at home.

*"My best advice, whether you've been a long-distance parent for a week or ten years, is **do something!** Your child will be glad and so will you."*
GEORGE NEWMAN

In his blogpost 'Divorce & Long Distance Parenting: How to Cope With Being Away' on www.fatherly.com in June 2018, Chris Illuminati writes that with some guidance and out of the box thinking, these 'Live-Away Dads' can still have a considerable influence over their children. He quotes Dr Racine Henry, a licensed Family Therapist: "Regardless of the circumstances surrounding Dad's absence, a bond with their child will be unbreakable when it includes special things that are unique to their relationship, whether it's an inside joke, special names for one another, a story that you both write together line by line whenever you speak, the important thing is to give the child something to look forward to that is unfailing."

William Klatte wrote a book called *Live-Away Dads* about what dads can do after a divorce. He emphasises the importance of keeping your promises, showing your kids that you are going to be okay, supporting their mum, being the best parent you can be and being involved for the long haul. These are principles that parents who travel a lot for work or who are living far from their family can put into practice too.

"Affirming words from moms and dads are like light switches. Speak a word of affirmation at the right moment in a child's life and it's like lighting up a whole roomful of possibilities."
GARY SMALLEY

Dr Ken Canfield is a researcher specialising in fatherhood. He is founder and president of the National Center for Fathering – a non-profit education and research centre dedicated to inspiring and equipping men to be responsible fathers. From his years of research, he developed the programme called 'I CAN', which stands for 'Involvement, Consistency, Awareness, and Nurturing.

In his article for *Charisma Magazine*, entitled 'Long-Distance Fathering: Making the Most of a Difficult Situation', Dr Canfield writes this about consistency: "Be regular and predictable in your emotions, your schedule, and in keeping promises." He goes on with examples of Awareness and Nurturing: "Maintain an awareness: get feedback as often as you can about your children. Talk to teachers and coaches and keep track of each child's individual needs and concerns. Make sure you physically nurture them when you're with them, but also do it verbally as often as you can. Instead of being lavish with new toys or other gifts, shower them with displays and words of affection. Affirm your kids for who they are and for what they were created to be."

Colleen Higgs shares a cracking example of how her husband manages to engage their young children over the phone: "He kicks off Skype calls with chopsticks sticking out of his nose. He pretends all is normal while the kids yell, point and tell him he needs to do something about those chopsticks!" Silliness is a wonderful way to connect. Sitting still and talking to a screen is hard for little ones. Playing a game could work if you both have a board or can give directions when it's Dad's turn.

Silliness is a wonderful way to connect.

Valentina, whose husband went to Morocco ahead of her to set up their new family home, has more ideas. When borders closed due to the coronavirus pandemic in early 2020, Valentina and her children were unable to join him. She shares the following list of ideas:

- I send their dad screenshots of schoolwork and he helps them with online school.
- He teaches them online how to brush their teeth.
- The children and their dad use drawing apps that allow them to draw together. I won't share with you what I looked like the last time they drew me.
- The most important for me was to Skype while indoors. Every time he was outdoors (pretty much the whole lockdown), it made us feel that he had a great life and freedom. I asked him not to be so

annoyingly positive. It makes us/me feel that he is happy and having a beautiful life without us/me. Now he is learning how to talk to us with a normal, everyday face.

Noelle also shares from her experience: "In playful moments, my husband loves to send challenges based on his context to our children (find something hidden on a picture, discover the name of a country based on the flag, find the name of a strange fruit, and so on). When it comes to education, I find it more difficult. We discuss the problems. Together, we take what we consider to be the best decision. If necessary, my husband will speak with our children to give the message, so I feel supported (that's important with unpopular decisions)."

If you are raising your children in multiple languages, being away on a work trip can still allow for fun games that foster the language that you share with your child. *The Toolbox for Multilingual Families*, by Ute Limacher-Riebold and Ana Elisa Miranda, is jam-packed with activities to foster children's speaking, understanding, reading and writing skills.

How to talk to teens over the phone when you are away

Child Psychologist Shelja Sen offers advice when entering into conversation with teenagers.

First, avoid saying 'let's talk': "When we say 'let's talk' to our teenagers, alarm bells go off in their brains and the shutters come down," she writes in her article '5 Simple Tips to Help you Have a Real Conversation with a Teen' on ideas.ted.com in January 2018.

Then, ask, don't tell and respond from the heart. This is something that works well on the phone. Asking teens about their opinions on a world event or family situation, really listening to their answers and responding to them, will open communication. Join them in their world rather than expecting them to join yours. "When we empathize from our hearts, teens won't feel blamed, shamed or judged, which makes them more likely to open up to us."

The You-I-We approach works well too, even at a distance. This is how Shelja Sen explains it: "I listen to **You** and understand your perspective (even if I do not agree with it). **I** share my perspective as a parent (even if you do not agree with it). Then **We** sort this out together."

Last but not least, apologise if you mess up, which is also pretty feasible from miles away.

The Constant Parent

"Before I got married, I had six theories about bringing up children. Now, I have six children and no theories."
ANONYMOUS

Include the absent parent

Owen Kibenge goes on to share during his NPR interview how helpful it is when other family members reinforce his relationship with his daughter. His daughter's grandmother and his wife encourage her to make sure she calls him if something fun has happened in her life. He is responsible for the discipline side of things too and is often the trump card when she may not be doing what she's supposed to.

> "I would keep his toothbrush and toothpaste that lived in our Swiss apartment. He also had half the closet space. So, when he got there, he had **his** stuff. It wasn't like a stranger coming into the apartment, it was like 'you **fit** here.'"
> SUNDAE SCHNEIDER-BEAN

Talking about them, keeping their wardrobe space 'open' in the closet, having their toothbrush in the bathroom, also means that their presence is being felt. When we are on a car trip, we normally take it in turns to choose songs. The other day, even though it was just the boys and I, we decided to give Olivier his turn. Although he was away, he felt present. Sundae Schneider-Bean shares about the time she and her boys lived in a separate country from her husband: "I would include my husband in the everyday, like sending a picture of a lost tooth or the boys on the swings. Even if he didn't respond, I still sent images throughout the day, so then if he did talk to them, he'd be able to say 'Oh, I saw that you were at the park today' or 'I know you lost a tooth.' He could show to the children that he knew what was going on in their lives."

One small addition with huge impact can be to have a second clock in the living room, set to the time where 'Dad' or 'Mum' is.

"Look, it's 12 o'clock where Daddy is. He must be having lunch now," or "Papa is in bed now, please don't send him an SMS, you'll wake him up," we can tell our children so they can visualise him.

LONDON **NEW YORK**

Regina, a mother with very young children, shares how she involves Dad:

- Zooming at mealtimes. Sometimes kids eat while I clean dishes. Dad is with them online.
- Quality one-to-one calls. Allowing my older child to sit with headphones in a different room and talk to Dad about anything special.
- Documenting progress in learning, artwork, anything special and sending it to Dad, then he sends his reaction as a voice message or video.

- Recorded stories, fairy tales by Dad which can be played at bedtime.
- Talking about Dad's work, why he is away. Allowing big emotions to unwrap is very important. Accepting these emotions, letting your child cry, grieve and allowing hurtful words like: "I don't love you, I will hit you when you come back" (understanding that it is because they love their Dad so much, it hurts so much that he left) and explaining it to Dad as well.
- Praying for him and explaining that he is working hard to provide for us; it's hard for him too, to be away from us.
- My husband orders gifts for the kids from time to time and I record videos of how the kids received them.
- Looking forward to the date of a reunion, a countdown, planning special things when he is back, making a celebration, baking a cake for Dad.
- Pulling the invisible rope that connects heart to heart, whenever a child misses Dad.
- Preparing handmade gifts for Dad.
- Playing sport together. Letting kids coach Dad. Recording sport achievements especially for him.

Pull the invisible rope that
connects heart to heart, whenever
a child misses Dad.

It's hard not to wonder sometimes if parents who are away for work are damaging their children by their absence. "Children communicate principally through behaviour," explains Dawn Purver. "Therefore, parents need to continually hold curiosity about the message that the child is communicating and wanting to be understood by the parents, via their behaviours; both positive and negative. Behaviour is often the window into how a child is coping, so notice and pay attention to any changes that indicate the child needs something more from the parents." Both parents can discuss behavioural change. The one 'at home' will obviously be the one who can observe the said behaviour but they can also involve the other parent by asking them to be vigilant about requesting regular feedback on how a child is acting.

Day-to-day parenting

"I am finding it hard to be the only adult around, let alone the only parent – I'm exhausted," I admit to myself after one particularly brutal Saturday where I have been trying to do chores, run errands, take the boys on an outing in the sunshine, fix the bathroom drain, cook meals and referee two bickering boys.

Three kinds of parenting

I realise there are three kinds of situations in parenting.

1. Proactive parenting
We can do some aspects of this together. Proactive parenting is about discussing values we want to live by and instil in our children, family mottos and atmosphere, pocket money and education. Things like that.

2. Implementation parenting
But when it comes down to the nitty-gritty of parenting, well, that's down to the parent who lives with the children. Not only does it require being intentional in the reaction to what is going on but also being intentional in the implementation of the discussions you and your partner have had together.

My husband helps me with the implementation process, and even simple reminders help (for example, I always forget to give them their pocket money on time; he is responsible for reminding me).

"Have you brushed your teeth yet?" I ask, in the high hopes that this pre-bedtime ritual has been done. The boys aren't two years old anymore. They technically should be able to accomplish this on their own.

"Done!" I hear both boys call out.

"How long did you brush for?"

Silence.

Well, that is all I need to know. I can safely assume that the two minutes of brushing didn't happen... (we got told off by the dentist for not brushing teeth long enough). No matter how much I discuss teeth brushing with my husband, the responsibility of getting the brushing *actually done* lies with me. And this is what I am now finding exhausting. Because it is not only about mouth hygiene, it is about sibling rivalry and bickering, about how much TV they watch and when they need to go out and play. It is about whether they are practising their German words or Maths or piano. It is about making sure they take their signed paperwork back to school and the money they owe for a trip or something.

3. Responsive parenting
Something happens in the family and I am the sole parent involved at that very moment. I need to decide how to respond, what to say, decide if consequences are appropriate and yes, decide how to implement them. I have learnt that I can defer some of these responses until "Papa and I have discussed them together". Other situations, however, fall on me and me alone to sort out there and then.

If your life partner is frequently away from home for work, you may feel a lot of the time like a single mother.

One parent in the 'Holding the Fort Abroad Survey' describes the challenge this way: "I need more time for the morning routine to get children ready for school without his help and we adjust dinner time to be sure to eat when he can be home from work." Another mentions school runs as well: "School runs for kids (I work at their school but usually go in earlier and return later). Having responsibility for getting the kids to and from school = more work at home in the evenings + very early morning (before they are awake)."

But the truth of the matter is, you are not a single parent. Your spouse, your life partner, however you want to describe the 'other' parent, is 'only' physically absent. Unless your partner has withdrawn from parenting altogether, which is a totally different conversation, then you are both in this parenting gig together. As solo parents, however, we can learn so much from single parents and adapt what they put in place regarding parenting to some of what we live on a daily basis.

There are parts of Kathlene Seney-Williams's book *Surviving and Thriving on the Single-Parent Journey* that we will be able to identify with, including:

- You are doing most of the disciplining and all the school runs.
- If there is an emergency during school time or your child is sick, you are on call.
- You can't just bury your head under the duvet if you are having an off day.

I was about to add to that list:

- You can't ask the other parent to call your child out if a boundary is crossed.

Well, this last point illustrates what I mean when I say that we are not single parents, because we can involve the other parent when boundaries are crossed. This is even possible when co-parenting (when both parents are parenting although they are no longer in a relationship together). Who says I can't ask my husband to hold my child accountable for a behaviour even if he is not physically present?

One day, I realised that I was parenting from the wrong default setting. When something comes up at home,

I will normally automatically tell myself that I can handle it, without even wondering whether it would be an opportunity for Olivier to take part. I have to stop myself and ask: is distance a good enough reason for my partner not to be involved in parenting this with me? Maybe our partner can even take a lead in responding.

I am finding that there are many opportunities for him to be involved. It might not be necessary for shorter trips, but for longer trips, if time differences permit, he can call the children in the evening to check if they have brushed their teeth. He can stay on top of holding children accountable for clean rooms or managing their screen time. The trick is to delegate this to our partners and not assume they can't get involved because of distance.

Is distance a good enough reason for my partner not to be involved in parenting this with me?

Involve the children

I once wrote in the 'Solo Parenting Expat Mums' private Facebook group that most of my time was swallowed up taking care of the children. One of the comments I got was to not shy away from involving the children. This is still a work in progress in our household as I find that sometimes I don't have the emotional or physical energy to actually get them to do some of the household chores. We are trying to instill some sort of chore routine while my husband is back, in the hope that the boys will have set jobs around the house they are used to doing.

Build traditions and routines

I'm not much of a routine person. Ask my family or my Virtual Assistant and they'd say I'm more of the 'hyper flexible' type. One distinction that has helped me though is having routines for the week and traditions for the weekend.

Karen explains how a routine during the day helps her a lot as she solo parents: "I get up in the morning at a certain time, then sit down and eat my breakfast, then sit down and eat lunch. We always sit down as a family to dinner. Then it's bath time. All the children have a bedtime. So the oldest one goes to bed at half past ten, the other one goes at ten, the other half past nine, the other one at nine, the next one at half past eight. So that is my foundation of discipline. Every Sunday is a family lunch. We sit around the table and we eat together and we talk, no phones, no cell phones, no laptops are allowed, even if the older teenagers kick and scream about it. After Sunday lunch, they can go out if they want to meet friends. Those older children are now young adults and share a house in Dublin. Do you know what they do? They have a roast dinner, every Sunday."

Andrea Schmitt shares a few insights on raising girls if their father travels frequently for work:

She and her husband have been travelling the world together for 25 years. In total she has 26 moves under her belt. She provides a safe space for girls 13–21 to voice their concerns, talk about their problems, set goals and make the most of their moves. When their daughter turned one, her husband started travelling three out of four weeks. I spoke with Andrea and her daughter, Jessica.

Andrea shares: "It is a roller coaster ride as you adjust to them being away, and then have to adjust again when they come back, and then away again."

"The fact that he was away wasn't weird," exclaims Jessica, laughing. "It was when he was at home that it was strange. I had to get used to him physically being there again, because it was mostly Mum and I."

Growing up with a travelling father was Jessica's norm. She realises, with hindsight, that her mum and dad were intentional about her always having a connection with him. Every evening, she would ask him for a funny story from his day, which they still do to this day. When he was home, her mum would pretend to have something to do so that father/daughter time would take place naturally. "We would sit in front of a movie and eat things my mum wouldn't normally let me eat," says Jessica. She laughs. As Jessica grew older, her father took her for weekends away, when she admits she learned a lot about him. We forget our children will not know our husbands as we do.

Special school events were attended by her mum, and those where her father was present were made all the more special because they were rarer. She vividly remembers the Daddy/daughter dance he took her to when she was five. "I can still remember the dress I wore and what a special day it was." Jessica is now a vivacious 22-year-old, confident, friendly and ambitious. She and her father have a special bond now that she is an adult. "He's more like a friend."

With younger children, survival mode is okay

"I think moms, single or not, put a lot of pressure on ourselves trying to balance it all. It's NEVER going to be perfectly balanced – the sooner you know this, the sooner you can relieve some of the pressure you put on yourself."
DENISE RICHARDS

When living in Dubai, Mariam's children were younger and when her husband travelled a lot, she was in "pure survival mode": "The only goal was to get through his travel and maintain some sense of sanity. We never really did that much with the kids because they were too young. And to be honest, with FaceTime, I couldn't schedule one more thing. I knew I was going to be by myself and I just had to get on with it. I didn't have the time to organize everything and coordinate. I just literally had to focus on the job at hand and make it through the day, through the week or the month or whatever it was. Yeah. It's hard."

Ute Limacher-Riebold knows what it is like to have young children and a travelling husband. At the time, she had three children under the age of four, the youngest being twins. "Parents need to know that it is okay if they don't want to go to certain places like the swimming pool as the only supervising adult," she says. She would organise outings with friends to work around that dilemma or stick to going to places where it was safe.

Beware of parentification

When a parent is the only adult in the home, they may end up leaning more on one of their children for emotional or practical support than they should do. It goes beyond asking a child to do chores and participating in the functioning of a family. It refers to a situation where "the adult essentially adopts the dependent position in the parent-child relationship, and in turn the child is expected to fulfill what are typically considered to be adult responsibilities" says Jennifer A Engelhardt in 'The Developmental Implications of Parentification: Effects on Childhood Attachment' published in the *Graduate Student Journal of Psychology* in 2012. Engelhardt has identified two types of parentification.

Two types of parentification

- Instrumental parentification "refers to the assigning of functional responsibilities to children, such as shopping, paying bills, cooking meals for the family, and taking care of the general logistics of running a household", going beyond a parent requiring a child to do 'chores'.
- Emotional parentification, according to Engelhardt, is the more detrimental of the two. It "requires

the child to fulfill specific emotional and/or psychological needs of a parent and is more often destructive for child development than instrumental parentification." This is a situation a solo parent may slip into without meaning to.

I have noticed that in our family, although I don't abdicate my role as a parent, I have to watch that I don't involuntarily let our oldest child slip into the position of 'dad', for example.

Include other adults

As you look to build a team around for your personal support, check who can help with the children.

Have a back-up adult

What if your partner is away and an emergency happens? Mariam Ottimofiore suggests having an adult you can call upon, someone you have pre-arranged would help. "It just makes sense that if you take out one adult from the equation, to make sure that you have a backup adult in case you need this person." She and her husband learned this the hard way when she broke her leg minutes before her husband was due to leave on an international flight. He was forced to delay his journey as they had no pre-arranged help. "First thing I did when arriving in Ghana," she says, "is arrange for back-up help immediately."

Role models

I watched with a twinge of sadness as the father-son duo cycled past me in the car one day.

My boys won't get to do that with their dad for a while, I thought to myself. Again, the same twinge, as I took them out that evening to kick a ball around. It reminded me of a book I read a while ago that had a big impact on me and that I want to re-read: *Strong Mothers, Strong Sons*, by a paediatrician and mother of four, Meg Meeker. She writes: "The truth is, no one can be both Mom and Dad. A woman can only be Mom, and believe me, this is good enough. So many single mothers exhaust themselves with worry and trying to be something that they can't be. Yes, a boy needs male influence, so rather than attempting to be a substitute yourself, recruit a good man or two to help you." I am going to hatch a plan to involve the adult sons of a family we are friendly with. Maybe they can play online with my boys and kick a ball.

Our teenager son made an interesting observation the other day when I mentioned this topic to him.

"I don't like to show my emotions because others don't," he said.

This, in my opinion, brings the conversation back to the importance of having grown up men (in movies, books, sports or real life) who model to our boys it is okay to cry when hurt, to show sadness or that they have been moved by something.

A boy needs male influence, so rather than attempting to be a substitute yourself, recruit a good man or two to help you.

When I asked for names of possible role models on my Facebook page, Roger Federer, Martin Luther King, David Beckham and Barack Obama popped up amongst others. Some named men they knew in their lives. Someone observed that we often talk about role models for girls but rarely for boys. Joanne Mutter points out in her 2017 Doctorate Thesis, 'The Impact of Contemporary Global Mobility on the Family who Stays Behind', that all travelling in the families she interviewed was done by the dads, and their boys seem to have had the hardest time when they were away.

Have fun

"When they look back on their childhood, it probably won't be the expensive trainers you bought them that your kids will remember. It'll be the time you made a tent in the lounge out of old sheets and camped out in it in sleeping bags overnight, telling each other stories, and eating snacks by torchlight," writes Kathlene Seney-Williams in her book *Surviving and Thriving on the Single-Parent Journey* and it is so true for any family situation. Let's remember to have fun with our children and create memories.

Transition Times

Dan Verdick warns about the adjustment time needed when coming home. "Don't be surprised if older kids initially have emotional reactions you don't expect [...] your child may seem shy, overjoyed, angry, or indifferent. No matter what the reaction, respond with extra love and sensitivity. Remember this is one more reason to maintain emotional connections with your child each time you're away for business." He also suggests rescheduling celebrations for when you return home.

"My husband helps a lot when he comes home," shares Colleen. "He's actually got the higher energy. But what happens is, he comes back and is all gung-ho to reorganise and make us all efficient. He's used to running his team like a tight ship. I need to remind him this is home, not an engineering project. Yes, we are inefficient and imprecise. These are children and we are a family. The other thing is that his priority about being efficient is not the same as mine. It helps to explain which things matter most to me and which I choose to let drop. I also need to remember to ask what matters most to him. This can help get on the same page." She also adds that he makes sure he gets some one-on-one time with each child within the first few days of being home. Lawyer, Mediator, Psychotherapist and twice expatriate Phyllis Adler echoes this sentiment in the hilarious piece 'My Friend Godzilla', reprinted in the book *Forced to Fly*, about what happens when her husband comes home after a business trip. She writes: "We are made to feel like failures in self-management. And if anyone knows about management, it's Godzilla." She goes on to explain that she finally understood that all her husband's attempts at reorganising the family were because he wanted to feel part of it again. She also told him what he was doing was not helpful.

It is important to clarify expectations around coming home. At one point, I expected my husband to relieve me of household chores and family duties. When he didn't immediately do so, I would get frustrated. How dare he not guess what I wanted him to take over?

One mum in the Facebook group also acknowledges that although she and her husband instantly reconnect, she has to consciously 'make space' for him to parent again in the family. And one travelling mum consciously takes a longer route to come home to give herself time to prepare to 're-enter' family life. "My head may be full of what I have been doing and the people I have met, but it is important for the travelling parent to take time with the children when they come home and ask them about their world," she writes. "My father frequently travelled. He would come in, I would jump in his arms but then he would put me down and say he needed to shower, change, and rest. He would then go on to do other things afterwards. He didn't know who my friends were or what was making me sad or glad. When I became a teenager, he was still trying to parent an eight-year-old."

"Saying goodbye again, explaining why you are going, using the last few minutes together to talk together about when you will see them next and what you will do is important," says Béatrice de Carpentier. *What do I tell them?* you might be wondering. *Will they think that they are less important to me than my job?* If the child expresses sadness or expresses an emotion about your departure, it is important to welcome their feelings. "Try verbalising their feelings for them," suggests Béatrice. "As you validate their feelings, pause; they will likely say something further about why they are sad. It may just be because they wanted **you** to take them to their soccer game. You may be able to find a solution to the dilemma that fulfills their need."

Karen shares what it was like when her husband first started leaving for a few weeks at a time. "At the beginning, you just don't know what to do with yourself. The whole pecking order gets thrown out of the window. The dynamics in the family change and the children see Dad's absence as a chance to change that order. Then there are transitions every time he flies back and reenters the family. My discipline and routine is different to his, then he steps back into the family three weeks later, asks why I am doing something a certain way and I have to explain that it suits me better. Then the children get upset and they say: 'that's not the way we do it when he is away. Why do we need to listen to him?' He's trying to be a loving husband, you are trying to be a loving wife. Timings change. It's incredibly stressful. He parented mostly when he was back but it wasn't much use. He was stepping into my world, into my 'office'. He could see much more easily when the children were pulling the wool over my eyes. He was spoiling their well-oiled techniques for getting what they wanted. In the beginning, I would just keep quiet and be very cross. But as time went on, I had to stand up and say to my husband: when you leave the pecking order changes and the longer you stay away, the longer that pecking order remains as it is. And then you come back and try to change it. You are going to have to look at it from a different perspective. As I have to look at it from a different perspective." Karen would sit her children down for a meeting as often and as regularly as the situation required, and issues were resolved.

Another mum highlights the discrepancies that show up sometimes between 'Mummy rules' when Daddy is away and the confusion that is created once her husband comes home and 'Daddy rules' suddenly also apply. She mentions the freedom she gives her children at the beach, to play with the sand and get it everywhere. For Daddy, finding sand in their nappies just stresses him out. Conversely, she is adamant the children have to clean up their Lego, whereas he is happy to leave it spread out on the floor of the play area. These differences would be apparent if both parents were parenting more or less simultaneously under the same roof but when one is frequently travelling, there is a delay in observing the differences in what is important for each parent. I have found that it can be extremely useful to not only communicate new or evolved rules with the travelling parent but also the steps to how these came about. These don't even have to be communicated on the phone, as your partner may be working long hours or be in a different time zone that makes it difficult to connect regularly. You may find a short email will do the trick for a quick summary.

Vici Tanner shares: "When he is away, we rarely communicate. We'll send the odd SMS and he may call and speak to the children but that's it. When he comes home and sees that I am irritated by something he did and I notice that he is finding it awkward to slot back into the family routine, then we communicate, a lot. We get things off our chest. It's obvious to us that we don't have a choice but to make things work."

Chapter 6
Split Locations: The Marathon

"If you want to run, run a mile. If you want to experience a different life, run a marathon."
EMIL ZÁTOPEK

Bern, Switzerland, March 2019
"I've just come off the phone with the Ambassador," Olivier informs me stepping into the kitchen.

I turn towards him and raise my eyebrows as an indication for him to give me more information about his call, without interrupting the circular movement of my wooden spoon in the soup I'm cooking for tonight's supper.

"He's brought up the job in Kabul again, the Director of Cooperation one he mentioned at Christmas. At the time, he said you and the boys would need to move to Dubai and me to Afghanistan. Do you remember the one? Now it looks like you could probably stay here."

I turn towards him, speechless. "Well, that is an interesting development! This whole 'living-in-two-different-countries' thing could actually be feasible."

"Are you sure? I wouldn't want it to be too hard for you and the boys. What about our parents? They are getting older."

"Olivier, this could work! Listen, every single job you've applied for in the past six months hasn't been right, either from our point of view or from theirs. You've always dreamt of going back to Kabul."

"That's true," he acknowledges.

"The kids have only just adjusted after our last move," I go on, getting into my stride. "It would be great for them to do this academic year here. I would be able to keep an eye on your parents and mine. I have good friends here. If you come back every six to eight weeks and spend as much of the school holidays as you can, then I think we can do it."

"We said we'd never do it. Look at us now."

"I know," I replied, smiling. "I'm sure there will be challenges ahead and it won't be easy, but I feel it is the right time and we can do it."

Over the following weeks as we were considering whether my husband would *actually* work abroad while I stayed with the kids in Switzerland, it really was about considering whether we wanted to live a different life. Little did we know – at the time – that many families do this. Olivier had had a few colleagues who would go on temporary assignments for six months as consultants while the rest of the family stayed in their 'main' home.

The other six months of the year were spent on personal projects. But those were the days, at the beginning of our marriage, when we had agreed we would never live apart.

Shortly after our initial conversation, I discover an acquaintance's husband has been living in a different country for a while already. The subject had never come up in our conversations before! The next time I see her, I mention it.

"I hear your husband is living in another country. Is that true?"

"Oh, yes! He commutes."

"He commutes?" I reply, surprised. "How often does he come home?"

"Every six weeks," she replies, waving her hand, as if dismissing it as no big deal.

Well, that's one way of looking at it!

Within two months, we have met half a dozen families who are currently in or have previously lived in what is called split family arrangements. Most of them attend the international church we go to. How on earth have we not talked with them about this before?

Why is it that this topic rarely comes up in conversation? After all, it's a massive deal.

If your husband or wife is away from home for longer periods of time, say six weeks and more, there will be some additional challenges to think about.

For some families, the assignment has an end in sight: a few months, a year, two years. For others, the situation may be open-ended. We met a South African couple who had lived long-distance for many years. She had raised the children in Ireland while he worked in Belgium for business for five years and in China for three years. He was able to fly home from China every eight weeks for one week. They are still very much in love and their children are thriving adults. They inspired me. *How did they do it?* I wondered. This section of the book includes the wisdom collected from these families.

The Decision

Rarely does a decision of this magnitude get taken quickly. Usually, the idea gets floated around for a bit while other alternatives are studied. My favourite analogy for this period of waiting is the beginning of a race when the runner is crouched in the start position.

"Ready, steady, wait... hold..."

And then we have to remain in that 'crouching' position for a while until we are told: "Go!"

It can get uncomfortable, can't it? If you have experienced this waiting period, this limbo, you know what I am talking about. Sometimes we need to keep a daily life functioning while waiting for quite a long time to know whether we will be taking this leap into a different life. You may also have to deal with false starts. Factor in the possibility of a rescheduled 'going-away' date, maybe even more than one.

This is a good time to reflect on what is important to you.

Reflect on motives

Yvonne McNulty and Kate Hutchings' study, 'Split Family Expatriation: Perspectives from expatriates and their career spouses', published in *ResearchGate* in April 2018, identifies reasons families decide one partner "works/lives in one country and their partner (and sometimes their children) live and work in another country." For many, having ageing parents is a huge factor in the arrangement. I stayed in a country where I am only an hour and a half's flight away from my mum, rather than a long-haul one. For others, it is to provide continuity for the children's schooling, or the job offer may be attractive financially and represent a big promotion. Some positions are necessary steps to management roles down the road. In our case, we cumulated all the reasons! One respondent from my 'Holding the Fort Abroad Survey' is based in Thailand. She writes: "Children have not had to move schools. I have been able to stay in my current job."

You may find it helpful to ask yourself the following questions:

- Am I doing it because I like a challenge? This can be a big one. If you are someone who likes adventure and thrives on being stretched, this might be an important question to ask yourself. There is nothing wrong with enjoying a challenge, but it might not be the best reason if it is the overriding one for going into this arrangement.

- Am I addicted to change and moves? This is another one that many Global Nomads wonder. It's the 'itchy feet' syndrome. In this case, it would be the change that would be attractive.
- Am I agreeing to this out of a sense of sacrifice because it will mean a good career move for my partner? It is crucial to consider whether you will resent them for it later.

Olivier had his own process of thinking about his motives and I am so grateful that we both reviewed what was motivating us to go ahead. It helped us clarify our intentions and have thought-through explanations when some members of our extended family inevitably questioned our motives.

The study 'What Motivates Successful Marathon Runners? The Role of Sex, Age, Education, and Training Experience in Polish Runners' published in *Frontiers in Psychology* in July 2019 gives insight into why people run marathons. Apart from the physical benefits (weight loss, health) that are not relevant here, goal achievement (that is "personal challenge and the sense of achievement") was the top motivator. It is one thing to want to run a marathon, it is another to drag the whole family into running one. If the family as a unit can look at this time apart as a joint, family project towards achieving one or more goals, it would help them succeed.

> It is one thing to want to run a marathon, it is another to drag the whole family into running one.

In their study 'Expatriate Family Narratives on International Mobility: Key Characteristics of the Successful Moveable Family' published in *Work and Family Interface in the International Career Context* in 2015, Mila Lazarova, Yvonne McNulty and Monica Semeniuk identify that the whole family "being on the same page" and "being committed to the move" are characteristics of a family successfully moving abroad. This would also contribute to a successful split family arrangement.

Reflect on vulnerabilities

There is no way that you will be able to anticipate all the needs you and the other members of your family will have along the way and where your vulnerabilities will lie. Let alone the fact that there will no doubt be surprises and changes. As much as possible though, it is well worth thinking ahead about emotional and practical support for yourself, for parenting together and for your relationship as a couple when your partner will be away for longer periods of time.

Just as a marathon runner will meticulously plan their nutrition, choose the shoes and socks they will wear depending on the terrain, and build a team around them to train with and cheer them on, so it should be with anyone who is about to launch into a longer-term separate living arrangement from their life partner. In 'How to run a marathon – free marathon training plans for every kind of runner' for *Runner's World* in January 2019, Jane McGuire puts it this way: "If you're a complete beginner, it's best to start with a training plan focused on getting you round the course, not finishing in a certain time." This certainly applies to split family arrangements. The aim is to actually run the race.

Rope a friend in, someone who will not judge you but who will help you identify needs you may not have thought of. Speak to a Psychotherapist or a Certified Life Coach who is familiar with the global nomadic lifestyle. They will also be able to help you identify needs in advance. Review the first chapters of this book. Most of what they cover can be applied to longer times apart.

Expressing needs and expectations

There are three other areas useful to discuss before your partner is gone:

1. How will you make your needs known?
2. What expectations do you and your partner have about how your needs will be met?
3. How will you be mindful of your needs while your partner is gone?

Reflect on dreams

My husband had always dreamt of going back to Kabul. Living apart from his family was not by any means part of that dream to begin with. It just so happened that the job he was offered came at a time when it lined up with other life circumstances for our family and didn't clash with anyone else's dream. Again, one of the family characteristics that Lazarova's study identified for successful moveable families applies here: "All family members are treated as important and come first in family decisions." The aim is to figure out how *everyone* in the family can soar. This may involve some creativity and I would argue that the split family arrangement may turn out to be the answer to facilitating more than just one partner following their dream.

The aim is to figure out how
everyone in the family can soar.

Approach it like a project

"Key stakeholders can make or break the success of a project. Even if all the deliverables are met and the objectives are satisfied, if your key stakeholders aren't happy, nobody's happy."
ADRIENNE WATT

Consider this from a project management perspective. It is a project after all, with stakeholders: you and your partner, your children, certain members of your extended family, close friends will all be 'key stakeholders' in your family project. "Stakeholders are individuals who either care about or have a vested interest in your project.

They are the people who are actively involved with the work of the project or have something to either gain or lose as a result of the project," writes Adrienne Watt in her book *Project Management*. "A project is successful when it achieves its objectives and meets or exceeds the expectations of the stakeholders."

We have decided that our children would always know what decisions were being made regarding Olivier's job and any potential moves that would mean for us as a family. We do not want them to overhear us talking to friends or between ourselves and worry alone about what they heard. They need to feel part of the process. Their hopes and dreams need to be included in the mix. It can also teach them valuable life skills on living during times of uncertainty, decision-making, communicating needs and boundaries. Furthermore, we argue that knowing as soon as possible gives them more time to process instead of finding out just before the change. This is a personal decision. I know that some families prefer to tell the children once more concrete decisions have been taken in order to avoid putting the children through all the changes that may occur.

The Preparation

"Showing up begins long before you stand at the start."
GINA GREENLEE

Finally, the decision has been taken; your partner will be leaving. You may even have a date but for the moment, you are still in the same location. Time to move on to the next stage: preparing for a sustained amount of time when you will be apart.

Gina Greenlee is a three-time marathon runner, exercise physiologist and author. In her book *The Whole Person Guide to Your First Marathon*, she writes that once the decision has been taken, it is time to "move it from imagination to concrete action." But she wants us to play with the idea first, not plan to begin with. She's right. If your project is a family one, that is part of a dream, a goal, that doesn't negate others you care about, then there is no reason not to daydream about the possibilities it will offer, the fun it will be, the new adventure it suggests, and play around with how it can work out for real. Then the time will come to prepare.

Consider your relationships

You and your partner
The first relationship to warrant your attention is the one that you have with your partner. They will be physically absent from your home and you will not be seeing them 'in the flesh' for long periods of time. Reflecting on the following questions can be useful as you prepare together.

The first one helps you plan the time together you have left; the others are for you to discuss while you are still in the same location.
1. How and when will you spend time together before they leave?

2. How do you each feel 'held in mind' by the other person?
3. How do you share life while you are apart? How do you stay connected?
4. How often will you communicate? Be explicit. Will you make a point of saying 'good morning' and 'goodnight' to each other, even if that is the only exchange you have on certain days?
5. Do you want to write hand-written letters to each other? Use a secure app? Send photos of everyday life?
6. Would you like to exchange a personal item that the other can treasure while apart?

You can use the checklist in *Appendix 4* to keep track of your answers.

The children
The children may be quite young and not understand the implication of your partner being away for long periods of time. Joanne Mutter points out that children don't always have a notion of how long their parent has been away. Projecting a prolonged absence may be difficult for them. But there are still some things you can do to prepare.

1. Ask them if they would like to lend the parent who is leaving a stuffed toy or something precious. This won't be to 'remind' the parent of their children, but as a treasure from home.
2. Help them express any emotions they may be feeling about separation. "Encourage the child

to talk too, using a variety of ways to support them in articulating their feelings and thoughts: games, books, and so on appropriate for their age range. This will help them learn the emotional vocabulary to express their thoughts and feelings," shares Dawn Purver (see *Resources* for a list of books).

3. Ask them how they are going to communicate with you when they are worried.

I have also included the questions above as a checklist in *Appendix 4:*

Your network

As you are making your decision, you may not want too many people informed. People differ on the level of privacy they prefer. You and your partner may have different opinions on this! But once you take that decision and communicate it to your community, you may face many questions. Being clear on motives, needs and dreams will come in handy at this point.

This checklist may be helpful to keep on hand once the word gets out and friends start reaching out:

1. Keep track of who is offering what. Be specific. If a friend is offering you 'help' they will say something general like, "Give me a shout if you need anything." Make sure to have a discussion with them about *what* they could offer.
2. Ask certain people to check up on you. Many people will offer to be a 'listening ear' if you need

it but what are the odds that you will reach for the phone when you are in the middle of a crisis. Imagine how wonderful it will feel when, on a vulnerable day, a friend you have pre-arranged would check in with you on a regular basis (the important part being that *they* remember to call and ask how you are doing) actually calls for a catch-up. This might even prevent a crisis from becoming full-blown. They may be able to pre-empt what you need before you even have to ask for it.

Goodbyes

Your partner may be going back and forth from their 'work' country so you may feel that it is not necessary to organise them a leaving party. Reflect on whether this is something that would be helpful for them as they will be saying goodbye to friends for a long time. When they come home for a visit, they will likely not be able to catch up with all the friends they would like to. A leaving party also signals to family and friends that your partner *is* going to be absent. They aren't just leaving for a few days or weeks. If they are working in another country on a longer basis, they will be repeatedly absent and their home visits will most likely include some or many work visits to Headquarters (yes, sorry, you may not escape these), reconnecting with close family and friends and probably more trips to other countries to visit extended family if your family is already living a globally mobile life. This is another layer of complexity if you are both from different countries. With limited home visits, which 'home country' gets priority for an overseas trip?

Assess and communicate the risks

A risk is any uncertain event or condition that might affect your project. Let's not forget that some unexpected events might turn out to be opportunities!

It is worth looking risk squarely in the eye and trying to list the risks. Adrienne Watt outlines four basic ways of handling a risk. Look at ways to **Avoid** the risk, **Mitigate** it, that is reduce it somehow, **Transfer** it, mainly by taking out insurance, and finally, if none of the above are possible, **Accept** it. "But even when you accept a risk, at least you've considered the alternatives," she writes and have factored the risk into your planning.

We communicated to our children, in age-appropriate ways, the risks involved in their dad moving to Kabul adding that there were mitigating and emergency plans in place in case we need them. Karen and Tom would sit their children down for a meeting before Tom would leave for a new assignment. They would explain what the job was and ask the children how they felt about the situation. Sometimes the children would say something, sometimes they would sit silently, processing.

The Reconnections

Here is an excerpt from my diary written a few days after Olivier flew back for his first trip home:

Olivier is back, after nine weeks apart. It is the longest we have ever been apart in all our years of marriage. I could hardly sleep on Thursday night, knowing he was in the air on his return home. My stomach was in knots, my brain spinning with thoughts. What will our reunion be like? I wondered.

Now I find myself caught in between two opposing dynamics. I want to relax and enjoy our time together. After all, he will be off again in 18 days and he will probably be gone longer this time. He is in holiday mode. I, on the other hand, still have a long to-do list before the boys and I stop for the Christmas break. Maybe I should have planned it better? Maybe next time I will make sure there is space planned for both of us to relax together and work on a small to-do list together. Maybe my work needs to stop at the same time as his so we can fully enjoy the time together. To be continued...

Cindy and Luke lived in separate countries for a year when their children were young. They were the first couple we sat down with and peppered with questions when we were deciding whether to do it or not.

I am so grateful that Cindy warned me about being mindful when we reunite after the initial separation. "As your husband comes home, he will upset the routine and some rules, as he may not be aware of changes made in his absence. Just go with the flow," she advises. "He is also no longer used to living a family life and may have re-acquired bachelor reflexes. When he does something 'bachelor-style', communicate what that means for you." I think she saved us a huge amount of hassle. She was so right! Since then, other couples have warned us of this too as reuniting may not be as seamless as one might expect.

As your husband comes home, he will upset the routine.
[...] Just go with the flow.

I am amazed at how easily we fall back into all the old ways (by old, I mean the ways before his departure to live longer-term in a foreign country). He hasn't been back a day and we find ourselves falling back into the same routines, habits, dare I say it, ruts... But things have changed. Maybe I have changed? Or I see things more clearly now that I have had a chance to live differently for a while. This is the perfect opportunity to use the distance and spot the ruts you get back into when they come home.

We can learn a lot from military families who know what it's like to be in split locations. In a video entitled 'We Lived Two Parallel Lives' (see *Resources*), one family shares that when the dad came home from his first (13-month) deployment, he felt like a stranger. Learning lessons from their difficult reconnection, the family realised the importance of keeping him informed of what was going on in their daily lives, so during his second deployment they found creative ways to stay connected to Dad. The children organised a weekly 'family newsletter' that they would send him, where each family member would update him on new hobbies, changes to the household and anything important going on in their lives. He in turn would send them news on what was going on in his life. His return was definitely different the second time around.

I am convinced that it is not only vital to update your absent partner on changes in the family but also how some changes have been reached. When my husband sees a problem I am struggling with, I find it hard not to snap back when he 'suggests' something I should try.

"Why don't you try having dinner earlier?" he asks, trying to be helpful, if I am struggling with bedtime routine.

"I tried that, three weeks ago, when you were not around," I reply tersely.

Case in point. He is not aware of what I've already tried, what worked, what didn't and why we are doing what we are doing.

Some things will stay the same (I will always love a good John Grisham book), other things, for ourselves, our partners and our children, will change. Write up a list of things that have changed in the past week and see if you can start making categories (discipline, food preferences). You may think: *Why bother? Things will change again by the time they come home.* Communicating those changes as they come along will contribute to creating a family life over the miles and avoid 'family knowledge gaps' for the parent who was away. Now decide how you will communicate these changes. It could be in an ad hoc manner on the phone, in a newsletter like the family in the video, by email. Whatever works best for your situation.

Plan more than one date!
Once, Olivier returned home at Christmas time. After years of overly packed Christmas 'holidays', we had

finally figured out how to get a balance between planning time alone, time as a family and meeting up with friends, all while leaving enough margin for surprise guests and down-time. We had only planned one date for ourselves as time was short (he was back just two weeks and there were Christmas and New Year celebrations to fit in too). Of course, he fell sick on the day we had planned to have 'us' time. I was upset and frustrated. Finding the right time, the childminder, where we were going, what we were going to do, had taken some effort! These dates were few, far between and not so easy to organise.

I reminded myself that this was a learning opportunity. He was home, he needed rest, his body probably decided this was a good time to shut down for a bit and recuperate.

Lesson learned: make a margin for illness and plan *at least* two alone-time dates just in case one falls through for some reason.

A docking period

> "No marriage, or life, is static, however much we might wish that things would stay the same. People change. Some marriages can't handle transformations and growth."
> **PHYLLIS ADLER**

My husband calls the few days following his return to the family the 'docking period', like when a ship comes back to port. In 2006 a study called 'When long-distance relationships become geographically close' published in the *Journal of Social and Personal Relationships,* explored what happened once long-distance dating couples reunited. About half of the couples from the study didn't even get to experience this transition as they ended their relationships during the time apart. The study found that among reunited relationships, one-third terminated within three months of reunion. The authors write: "Participants' open-ended responses highlight changes associated with reunion, including the loss of autonomy; increased positive and negative knowledge; time management difficulties; and heightened conflict and jealousy." Most of us are way past the dating stage with our partners but that transition time when we reunite is something to watch out for.

The chances are that you and they have changed during the time of separation. Remember also that the partner who comes 'home' will be adjusting not only to being in a family setting again, but also to the culture the rest of the family has been living in the whole time they have been away – as pointed out by Christine Gerber Rutt in her interview on long-distance relationships for the *Expat Happy Hour* podcast with Sundae Schneider-Bean (episode 161).

Have a list of set questions

"What we may not realise is that, in many cases, the failure of a marriage stems not from an impossible situation but from the couple's inability to work things through."
PHYLLIS ADLER

To smooth the transition, we have decided to ask each other a set number of questions within the first few days of him arriving back home (we ask each other these questions each time he comes home).

He asks me:

- What can I help with (for the family and for you)?
- What is already planned that I need to know about?

I ask him:

- Do you feel included?
- What can I do that would help you feel included?
- What would you like to make sure we have in our calendar?

You are very welcome to use ours or you may want to find your own. You could even ask your partner, prior to them arriving home: "What questions would be good to ask each other when we transition back to living under the same roof?" You may be surprised at how open they are to suggesting questions.

Three ways to sabotage things

Olivier and I had an enlightening follow-up conversation about these questions. He pointed out that there were three ways of sabotaging their usefulness:

- By asking but not acting on what has been requested.

- By using it as manipulation. For example, by suggesting something that you know is a way of using your partner for your own gain.
- By answering what you think your partner wants to hear.

Continuity

You may be wondering if you should be rearranging your life when your partner comes home. *Should I drop all my plans and focus on the time they are home?*

Dr Pauline Boss was interviewed in November 2013 for an article entitled 'Orphan Spouse: How to Best Cope With Ambiguous Loss?' published on the website *Expatriate Connection*. She was asked whether the family should cancel all their activities to focus on the parent coming home. She emphatically replies: "No! Don't cancel the birthday party with the friends. This is true with the military families too. The military person would come home and say, 'Now I'm back, everything should go back to normal the way I remembered it.' Well, it can't. The children may have some plans, they must continue so the person who's coming back needs to fit into the family. He/she should not expect to be the king or the honored person for the day. Maybe a dinner or something to say 'Glad you're back!' but the family has to have some continuity."

Staying the Course

This is it. You and your family are committed to a posting and to a way of life. It is probably safe to say that not that many people around you are living away from their partner. Not even other expats in your location. If you haven't already, you may want to join the private Facebook group 'Solo Parenting Expat Mums' where we encourage each other and where you will find inspiration and tips. You are now part of a worldwide tribe that includes families of sailors, military personnel, businessmen and women, humanitarian workers. Some are already living life as expats, others are living in their home countries. We are all running this marathon on different continents, but nothing is stopping us from running together, even at a distance.

"Listen to your body, it could be that something is being depleted. Ask yourself how you can refuel."
SUNDAE SCHNEIDER-BEAN

This week I have been looking at endurance: keeping going, not giving up. We are all better at keeping going at some things more than others. So maybe a good place to start would be by asking yourself where you think you have endurance or where you find it harder? For example, I can write for hours, a really long time. I enjoy the process, I can focus. But the actual act of running, well, for that I don't have stamina at all. I keep planning to be a runner.

And then there are situations where you don't have a choice, you just have to keep on going, like living through the Covid-19 pandemic. That's when I created my private Facebook group for solo parenting expat mums. It is all about helping us have endurance and keep going.

Some days are harder or easier than others as well. How do you get through those days where you have to get through the difficult times?

Here are some tips to help with our endurance.

Shift the weight around

Imagine you are carrying parcels, and someone adds one to the pile in your arms. What would you do? It is highly likely that you would move the parcels around in order to enable you to carry the extra parcel better along with all the others. What are you doing now that you can move? Maybe do it at a different time of day.

Let go

Maybe it is time to put one of those parcels down... Is there anything that you can ask someone else to take on? Are you doing something that is actually someone else's responsibility, like in a Rescuer role in the Losing Triangle? What can wait? Is there anything you are doing to the standard that someone else is setting?

In his article published on www.medium.com in May 2020, Sean Kernan writes about the 'Four Habits of Discipline' his Navy SEAL dad taught him. During 'Hell Week', the harshest training week of training, "The people who succeed only look a few minutes in front of them. They don't worry about Thursday or Friday. They are only focused on each individual exercise. They get through it one thing at a time," he writes.

Make your own deadlines

This point may seem that it doesn't fit with only doing one task at a time, but it is complementary. We break down tasks into smaller chunks for big projects. At the day of writing this sentence, it is the 25th of May 2020. Covid-19 has meant that we have been in lockdown since March. Olivier and I don't know when we will see each other again. I am setting an artificial deadline for September 2020. I can work my way backwards from that date and create artificial milestones that I can keep aiming for. If he comes home before September, I will obviously be over the moon. If he does not, then I have a long enough perspective and a plan to last the distance.

Using what has worked in the past

Think about times when you have had to push through. What has helped? What habit can you bring back into your life?

Enjoy the view

DD Guttenplan wrote an article in *The Guardian* in August 2008 on 'How to run a marathon (and enjoy it)'. It was actually a reply to another article from someone who had thoroughly disliked his first marathon experience. One of the essential elements, according to

DD Guttenplan, is to run slower in order to "enjoy the scenery. And the crowds."

Have hope

Sheryl Sandberg's book *Option B: Facing Adversity, Building Resilience, and Finding Joy* is about grief. At one point, she mentions Permanence (my life will never be the same), Pervasiveness (my whole life is ruined) and Personalisation (it is my fault), that stem from the work of the Psychologist Martin Seligman on how we respond to negative things in our life. These three Ps could easily be transferred to living with travelling partners. We could be saying to ourselves: "my partner is always going to travel" (Permanence), "we are never a family, we never do anything together" (Pervasiveness) and "my partner is gone because they don't want to be home, they don't love me, they would rather be away" (Personalisation).

In my opinion, the overriding sentiment that helps overcome these three Ps is hope: "Each day brings new life, new strength, new dreams and new hope. May you find courage, confidence and hope to reach out for your dreams," writes Lailah Gifty Akita, author and founder of Smart Youth Volunteers Foundation.

Continual adjustments

"No matter how well you plan, your project can always encounter unexpected problems."
ADRIENNE WATT

Split Locations: The Marathon

"I can't do it," I mutter under my breath. "I just can't do it."

It is the beginning of February 2020. I have been sick for most of the month of January, have writing deadlines I've committed to, two close friends have moved away, Olivier has been gone four and a half weeks and he is still four and a half weeks from coming home. On top of all this, my practical support network has disintegrated. The lady who comes once a week to clean can't come anymore, the student who is helping with admin, translation work and practical help around the house has changed schedule so she can't come either. I want to give my mum extra support and the boys need a lot of attention. I am determined not to regress and stop looking after myself, because that's a recipe for disaster. There just isn't enough time in the day to attend to everything. The session with my therapist helps me get unstuck.

"Acknowledge the losses and your feelings around them," she encourages me.

As I voice my frustration and sadness, I feel a sense of release.

"What can be set up to renew your support structure?" she then asks. "Sometimes this may need to be done proactively. Take time to think about what you need now."

Together we review the categories of support: practical, virtual/admin, emotional, professional, spousal/partner support. We discuss my lack of social life and options for outings with friends. These are activities that replenish me. I can't remember the last time I went to a concert or for a drink. I made plans to go out with a friend and set out to find someone to help me with the housework.

Again, Gina Greenlee provides us with inspiration when she writes about a vital component in marathon running: surrounding yourself with people who will encourage you, not bring you down.

"Tap those people who will truly be by your side, not project on you their fears, obstacles or worries," she writes. "Your supporters are positive, upbeat, and will fill your proverbial balloon with helium."

It is quite likely that you are going to have to make adjustments to your support network. Maybe some relationships will strengthen while others will drift.

Fuel your commitment

The preparation work you did and the conversations you had before the decision for your partner to work away was taken pays off when life gets tough. I must admit that in my younger days I paid little attention to motivation. I either enjoyed doing something or I didn't. Sometimes, my ultimate goal played a role in whether I continued or not. (I distinctly remember stopping teacher training in my early twenties because there was no way being a teacher was my ultimate dream.) Knowing my *why* never occurred to me: it was underlying, therefore invisible, and not immediately accessible to my decision-making process. Now I know the power of motives in contributing to sticking with something (or not).

Split Locations: The Marathon

Carrie Cheadle is a Mental Skills Trainer for athletes. In her article called 'How Bad Do You Want It: Motivation vs. Commitment' published on her website in March 2017, she puts it this way: "Commitment is the decision to act on what motivates you. Motivation is the drive that fuels the commitment. Commitment makes it happen, but motivation can make it a lot more fun!"

Refuel

"Your body provides you with constant feedback that can help improve your running performance while minimizing biomechanical stress. Learn to differentiate between the discomfort of effort and the pain of injury. When you practice listening, you increase competence in persevering through the former and responding with respect and compassion to the latter."
GINA GREENLEE

This is a learning process for me. You may be in a place where you are much more aware of your body and the way life's experiences affect it. Sundae Schneider-Bean brought it up when I interviewed her around the topic of solo parenting. She explained how when she had just returned to Switzerland with her two boys while her husband stayed on in Burkina Faso, she had needed to visit a Naturopath. She is a trained Coach and knew the techniques to 'organise' and be mindful. Yet when she went for her visit, she realised how much tension was in her body. "It's like I was stuck in my body in fight or flight mode," she shared.

The importance of Gina's quote also lies in the difference between the discomfort of effort and the pain of injury. She is talking of physical pain and injury but this could very well apply to inner health and damage done there too. We need to make the distinction between what is stretching us in a healthy way, maybe forcing us to 'grow up', become more independent from our partners, change our ways of doing things, and what is breaking our spirit, crushing our joy and negatively impacting our relationships.

Be a team

"It's as if we're in a harness, we work alongside each other, just 300 miles apart."
DEMELZA POLDARK in *Poldark*

This quote from the TV show *Poldark* set off a weeklong reflection on long-distance couples in the 'Solo Parenting Expat Mums' Facebook group. I don't normally watch historical dramas but this one caught my attention. Captain Poldark comes home from war to his home in Cornwall, England, to find that his father has died and his fiancée is getting married to his cousin. In the course of rebuilding his father's business and estate, he falls in love and marries a young woman he takes in. In season four, he goes to London to be an MP in the House of Commons and his wife stays in Cornwall. In those days that was a fairly long journey and he is gone for months on end.

There are lots of little elements in the show that resonate with me and make me laugh. For example, at one point, he comes back after weeks of absence and asks his wife what she has been up to. She gets really cross because she has been working like crazy keeping everything together on her own... sounds familiar.

Apart from the imagery of being oxen tied together – which isn't exactly how I imagine Olivier and I – it made me think about what is important to make couple life work when living apart.

Live and act as if you are living together. Continue to lean on each other instead of turning to someone who may be more physically near. One idea I saw was to have photos around of you both together. It's symbolic as much as anything. You might want to have a drink together one evening, read a book to each other or play a game of Scrabble 'on screen'.

Live and act as if you are living together.

Notice what kind of conversation you are having and make sure to include the 'date' ones and the 'relationship' ones.

Use the distance to your advantage

Why not work through Dr Gottman's Seven Principles together as we saw in *Use the Distance* in *Chapter 3*? You can certainly use the distance to rediscover each other and strengthen your friendship. The distance can also reveal the ruts you've got into as a couple. As you live apart, you may rediscover parts of yourself you had forgotten. This is also an opportunity for you to look at what you are doing, any personal development, where are you headed as an individual.

> The distance can reveal the ruts
> you have got into as a couple.

Create shared meaning

This is Dr Gottman's Principle Seven: 'Creating a shared sense of meaning'. Poldark and his wife were serving the poor together. They wanted to use the privilege they had in life to serve the less fortunate. When we were in New York, my husband was working on policy to protect displaced civilians during conflict. The numbers ran into the millions. How could I contribute to that? I realised though that we were working on two different levels: he was working on the macro level, with policies that could in fact change the lives of millions by encouraging governments to support certain groups of people. And I was working on the micro level: I could visit the lonely neighbour or volunteer at a homeless shelter. We still had a common purpose – serving those in need – but we were just doing it on two different levels.

How will you use the distance that you are experiencing at the moment? How will you be purposeful about creating a joint life? And what is the meaning or purpose that you both share?

Dr Boss, in an interview with *Expatriate Connection* published on September 13, 2013, suggests that if a split location needs to be, that then, "it's very essential for the partners to connect psychologically and physically in a predictive way".

The Final Stretch

"Where the marathon starts is after 30 kilometers. That's where you feel pain everywhere in your body. The muscles are really aching, and only the most prepared and well-organized athlete is going to do well after that."
ELIUD KIPCHOGE

For those families who have committed to a fixed-term long-distance contract, the final months can be taxing.

I certainly know that the way things are now, there's no way I'm able to actually run 20 miles, let alone a full marathon. Nevertheless, I'm amazed at how the principles of running can be helpful for a split location arrangement. Let's delve into how to manage those final months/weeks/days of an assignment that involved living separately. In a marathon context, the runners have given themselves completely and their bodies are exhausted, depleted. Sound familiar? Maybe we could borrow some of their techniques and use them for our final stretch.

Your state of mind

This is what Gina Greenlee writes in a chapter entitled 'Mile 20' in a journal entry called 'The Wall'. This is when most runners struggle. She writes: "My most negative. From many sources I read how the last six are killers no matter what shape you are in." Her knee is hurting, she has mental fatigue, she considers giving up, but then at mile 22, she starts talking herself in.

Could this be true of us after a long period of separation? We've been in good shape, we've parented the children and taken care of ourselves, we've put in all that support network and fielded all the unexpected 'stuff' that came our way. Now there's an end date just around that corner. Surely, we are elated, we've done so well up to now. Yet those last weeks can be the hardest. We're suddenly more aware of how much this journey has asked of us.

"This is where your mental training will pay off," writes Gina. "If you have nurtured your Spirit and trained your Mind as well as your Body, you'll be prepared with everything you need to draft across the finish."

I vividly remember a conversation with a friend who has a 16-year-old son. He commented that his son physically has the capacity to hike further than him, but he, the father, has the mental strength and therefore ends up going further. This shows how far our mental state can carry us, or not.

I looked up some running mantras out of curiosity and here are two:

"I was strong enough to get this far. I am strong enough to keep going."

"It is all in the mind."

I wonder how you feel about using those mantras when you hit a wall. Have you ever stopped yourself, captured your thoughts and purposefully changed them?

Eye on the prize

It was a wonderful privilege to listen to Karen as she shared her family adventures over the last 17 years, during which her husband travelled for various amounts of time for work. Together they have seven children, all now settled and successful. She shared: "In tough times, you have to remember why you are together, how you met. Think about the love you felt for each other. Keep coming to that in times when you are feeling incredibly challenged. Keep your eye on that ball. When you met, you would have had conversations about what your aspirations were, what you enjoyed together. There is light at the end of the tunnel." This is a wonderful reminder to focus on why you started this whole adventure in the first place.

Lessons learnt

Just like with any project at work, we are taught to debrief at the end, so we can figure out what worked and what didn't during our time living apart. If living in separate countries from your partner is part of your lifestyle and isn't a fixed-term appointment, then setting regular intervals at which to take stock can be useful. And don't forget to celebrate!

Special Thanks

I am so grateful to the following people who have contributed their expertise, their experience, their time and their stories to the making of this book. If you would like to get in touch with any of them for help in their specific area of expertise, their websites or Facebook groups are noted under their names.

Béatrice de Carpentier
https://bdecarpentier.alwaysdata.net

Helen Ellis
www.distancefamilies.com

Sharoya Ham
www.embracebehaviorchange.com

Colleen Higgs
https://colleenhiggs.com

Annabelle Humanes
www.thepiripirilexicon.com

Ute Limacher-Riebold
www.utesinternationallounge.com

Mariam Ottimofiore
www.andthenwemovedto.com

Dawn Purver
www.internationaltherapistdirectory.com

Carolyn Parse Rizzo
www.intervallifecoach.com

Andrea Schmitt
www.globalgirlcoach.com

Sundae Schneider-Bean
www.sundaebean.com

Vici Tanner
www.victoriatanner.com

Resources

'Solo Parenting Expat Mums'

- ✓ Strengthen your long-distance marriage.
- ✓ Parent together, even at a distance.
- ✓ Resolve hidden conflicts in your intercultural marriage.
- ✓ Reconnect smoothly after a business trip.

Join the community or just sign up for the Newsletter:

www.amulticulturallife.com

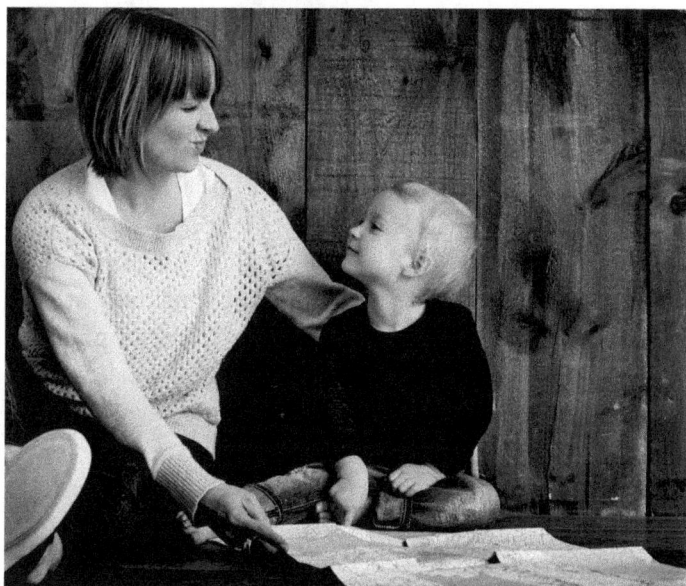

For the 'Holding the Fort' Partner

www.workaway.info is an online platform that allows people who want to swap their services for room and board in another country to connect with people who need help.

'The *Laws of Life* Essay Toolkit', Sherry Hamby, Victoria Banyard, Matthew Hagler, Wojciech Kaczkowski, Elizabeth Taylor, Lindsey Roberts & John Grych, *Life Paths Research Program*: https://www.lifepathsresearch. org/wp-content/uploads/Laws-of-Life-Toolkit-Hamby-et-al-2015-2.pdf

The Portable Business Accelerator, Tandem Nomads: www.tandemnomads.com/pba

Official Myers-Briggs test and personality assessment, MBTIonline: www.mbtionline.com

'Episode 3: Overcoming Loneliness Abroad', *The Empowered Expat Wife*, podcast: www.camillaquintana.com/podcast/episode3

'Dual career couples and putting the business at the same level as the partner's job', *Tandem Nomads*, podcast: https://tandemnomads.com/podcast/tn168-dual-career-couples-putting-the-business-at-the-same-level-as-the-partners-job/

'These Boots: A spouse's guide to stepping up and standing tall during deployment', *Military OneSource*, 2006:
http://dmna.ny.gov/family/theese_boots_mil_onesource.pdf

The Psychology of the Human-Animal Bond: A Resource for Clinicians and Researchers, Christopher Blazina, Güler Boyraz and David Shen-Miller (Eds.), Springer, 2011.

Mental Health

Expat Nest www.expatnest.com

Be Vocal: Speak Up for Mental Health is an initiative encouraging people across America to use their voice in support of mental health. *Be Vocal*, "aims to empower adults living with mental health conditions to speak up when talking with their professional support team and to speak up as a community to advance mental health in America." Tips for Speaking Up:
https://www.bevocalspeakup.com/how-to-be-vocal-for-yourself.html

The International Therapist Directory (an online global listing of 250 professional therapists, counselors, psychologists, and psychiatrists in 35 countries):
www.internationaltherapistdirectory.com

World Federation for Mental Health:
https://wfmh.global/Publications/

Helplines:
https://www.therapyroute.com/article/helplines-suicide-hotlines-and-crisis-lines-from-around-the-world

For Couples

Through the Distance: I Exist in Two Places, Here and Where You Are, Aditya Chauhan, Independently Published, 2017 (book of poems)

The Gottman Institute provides live workshops and training materials for couples as well as therapy referrals through their Network: "It is our mission to reach out to families in order to help create and maintain greater love and health in relationships. Online training is also available for professionals." www.gottman.com

Q Cards: www.qcards.co.uk

Lexulous (Scrabble-type game you can even play via email if you can't be online at the same time): www.lexulous.com/

MSN Multiplayer (free online multiplayer games including chess, card games and board games): https://zone.msn.com/en/general/article/genmultiplayermadness.htm?intgid=hp_Nav_5

Pogo (free online games, such as dominoes and Monopoly): https://www.pogo.com/free-online-games?filters=free%2Cmultiplayer

Sundae Schneider-Bean, 'Long-Distance Survival Guide with Christine Gerber Rutt':
https://www.sundaebean.com/2020/02/03/161-long-distance-survival-guide-with-christine-gerber-rutt/

Sundae Schneider-Bean, 'Love on Lockdown: Part 1 with Christine Gerber Rutt':
https://www.sundaebean.com/2020/05/04/174-love-on-lockdown-part-1-with-christine-gerber-rutt/

Expat Nest www.expatnest.com

'Let's Talk: Parenting Abroad When The Partner Works Overseas', interview by Ute Limacher-Riebold:
https://www.youtube.com/watch?v=AuLnhw1LGCQ&feature=youtu.be

'Let's Talk: Beyond Surviving, Life Abroad with a Travelling Spouse', interview by Navine Eldesouki (Facebook Live), *Coffee with Expat Women*, Facebook group (become a member of the private Facebook group to watch)

Videos on *A Multicultural Life* (as of October 2020): 'It's a lot for one person!'; 'It's a Marathon'; 'You are a couple even if you live miles apart'; 'There is no time for what I need'; 'Include the parent working away from home' and 'Boys expressing emotions, not taking Dad's place and role models': www.amulticulturallife.com

Parenting

National Center for Fathering: www.fathers.com

The Dad Website: www.thedadwebsite.com

Embrace Behavior Change:
www.embracebehaviorchange.com

'83 Conversation Starters For You to Use with Kids and Teens', Kristi Wolfe, September 25 2014:
http://drkristiwolfe.com/conversation-starters/

Staying connected to the travelling parent

'We Lived Two Parallel Lives', Military Kids Connect:
https://militarykidsconnect.health.mil/Military-Life/Family

For Children

About expressing emotions

Overcoming Your Child's Fears and Worries: A Self-Help Guide Using Cognitive Behavioural Techniques, Cathy Creswell and Lucy Willetts, Robinson; UK ed., 2007

The Color Monster, Anna Llenas, Templar Publishing, 2016

Aroha's Way: A children's guide through emotions, Craig Phillips, Wildling Books, 2019

Little Monkey Calms Down, Michael S Dahl and Oriol Vidal, Picture Window Books, 2014

'World Mental Health Day: 50 Mighty Girl Books About Understanding and Managing Emotions', Katherine, *A Mighty Girl*, October 2020: https://www.amightygirl. com/blog?p=11449&fbclid=IwAR2YvNhsI-3tQmOuimQh N67mdcPYiBRvGd9D4Z4HbxL04YYDo9J0n44dh0c

Around grief

Badger's Parting Gifts, Susan Varley, Andersen Press, 1987

I Miss You: A First Look at Death, Pat Thomas, Wayland, 2009

Around separation

The Kissing Hand (Illustrated Edition), Audrey Penn, Tanglewood, 2020

Daddy Dolls: www.hugahero.com

Cultures

The Culture Map: Breaking Through the Invisible Boundaries of Global Business, Erin Meyer, PublicAffairs, 2014 (masterfully uncovers the subtleties of culture, how the differences affect business and how awareness of them transforms interactions)

When Cultures Collide, Richard D Lewis, Nicholas Brealey, 2005 (provides leaders and managers with practical strategies to embrace differences and successfully work across diverse business cultures)

Intercultural Marriage, Promises and Pitfalls, Dugan Romano, Nicholas Brealey, 2008 (a must-read for anyone who doesn't share a culture with their partner; she sets the scene beautifully in the first few chapters on how we interact with culture, then, as she weaves in personal stories, she addresses frequent challenges for intercultural partners)
The Interchange Institute: www.interchangeinstitute.org

Global DISC: www.icq.global/intercultural-disc

Other Resources

Workaway: www.workaway.info

The National Institute for Play: www.nifplay.org

Expat Happy Hour, podcast:
https://www.sundaebean.com/expat-happy-hour

Bibliography

Books

This Messy Mobile Life: How a Mola Can Help Globally Mobile Families Create a Life by Design, Mariam N Ottimofiore, Springtime Books, 2019

Ambiguous Loss: Learning to Live with Unresolved Grief, Pauline Boss, Harvard University Press, 2000

A Great Move: Surviving and Thriving in Your Expat Assignment, Katia Vlachos, LID Publishing, 2018

A Moveable Marriage: Relocate Your Relationship Without Breaking It, Robin Pascoe, Expatriate Press Limited, 2003

Assertiveness, How to Stand Up for Yourself and Still Win the Respect of Others, Judy Murphy, CreateSpace Independent Publishing Platform, 2011

A Game Free Life, Dr Stephen Karpman, Drama Triangle Publications, 2014

Self-Nurture: Learning to Care For Yourself as Effectively As You Care For Everyone Else, Alice Domar, Penguin Books, 2001

Organizing Solutions for People With ADHD: Tips and Tools to Help You Take Charge of Your Life and Get Organized, Susan Pinsky, Fair Winds Press, 2012

The Fun and Relaxing Adult Activity Book: With Easy Puzzles, Coloring Pages, Writing Activities, Brain Games and Much More, Lomic Books, 2017

SAGE Handbook of Coaching, Tatiana Bachkirova, Gordon Spence and David Drake, SAGE, 2016

The 7 Habits of Highly Effective People, Stephen R Covey, Simon & Schuster, 2020

For Better: How the Surprising Science of Happy Couples Can Help Your Marriage Succeed, Tara Parker-Pope, Plume, 2011

The Seven Principles for Making Marriage Work: A Practical Guide from the Country's Foremost Relationship Expert, John Gottman and Nan Silver, Harmony, 2015

Couples That Work: How to Thrive in Love and at Work, Jennifer Petriglieri, Harvard Business Review Press, 2019

When Cultures Collide: Leading Across Cultures, Richard D Lewis, Nicholas Brealey, 2018

Beyond Culture, Edward T Hall, Anchor Books, 1976

The Culture Map: Breaking Through the Invisible Boundaries of Global Business, Erin Meyer, PublicAffairs, 2014

Expat Life: Slice by Slice, Apple Gidley, Summertime Publishing, 2012

Bibliography

Parental Guidance: Long Distance Care for Aging Parents, Ana McGinley, CreateSpace, 2016

The Business Traveling Parent: How to Stay Close to Your Kids When You're Far Away, Dan Verdick, Gryphon House, 2000

101 Ways to be a Long-Distance Super Dad or Mom, Too, George Newman, Blossom Valley Press, 2006

Live-Away Dads: Staying a Part of Your Children's Lives When They Aren't a Part of Your Home, William C Klatte, Penguin Books, 1999

The Toolbox for Multilingual Families, Ute Limacher-Riebold and Ana Elisa Miranda, 2020

Surviving and Thriving on the Single-Parent Journey: A Step-By-Step Approach, Kathlene Seney-Williams, Lion Books, 2019

Strong Mothers, Strong Sons: Lessons Mothers Need to Raise Extraordinary Men, Meg Meeker, Ballantine Books, 2015

Forced to Fly: An Anthology of Writing That Will Make You See the Funny Side of Living Abroad, Jo Parfitt (Ed.), Summertime Publishing, 2012

Project Management, Adrienne Watt, BCcampus Open Education: https://opentextbc.ca/projectmanagement/

The Whole Person Guide to Your First Marathon: A Mind, Body, Spirit Companion, Gina Greenlee, 2013

Option B: Facing Adversity, Building Resilience, and Finding Joy, Sheryl Sandberg and Adam Grant, WH Allen, 2017

Studies

'Managing Stress in the Expatriate Family: A Case Study of the State Department of the United States of America,' Amanda Wilkinson and Gangaram Singh, *Public Personnel Management*, 39 (20): 169-181

'The Winning Triangle', Acey Choy, *Transactional Analysis Journal*, 1990, 20 (1)

'The *Laws of Life* Essay Toolkit', Sherry Hamby, Victoria Banyard, Matthew Hagler, Wojciech Kaczkowski, Elizabeth Taylor, Lindsey Roberts & John Grych, *Life Paths Research Program*:
https://www.lifepathsresearch.org/wp-content/uploads/Laws-of-Life-Toolkit-Hamby-et-al-2015-2.pdf

'Predicting divorce among newlyweds from the first three minutes of a marital conflict discussion', Carrère S, Gottman JM, *Fam Process*, Fall 1999, 38 (3): 293-301

'Till stress do us part: the causes and consequences of expatriate divorce', Yvonne McNulty, *Journal of Global Mobility*, 2015, 3 (2): 106-136

Bibliography

'Production and Perception of Pauses in Speech', Kristina Lundholm Fors, *Semantic Scholar*, 2015: https://www.gu.se/en/news/pauses-can-make-or-break-a-conversation

'Talk is silver, silence is golden: a cross-cultural study on the usage of pauses in speech', Birgit Endrass, Matthias Rehm and Elisabeth Andre, *ResearchGate*, 2008: https://www.informatik.uni-augsburg.de/lehrstuehle/hcm/publications/2008-IUI-Endrass/endrass_et_al.pdf

'The Developmental Implications of Parentification: Effects on Childhood Attachment', Jennifer A Engelhardt, *Graduate Student Journal of Psychology*, 14, 2012

'The Impact of Contemporary Global Mobility on the Family who Stays Behind', Joanne Mutter, 2017: https://mro.massey.ac.nz/handle/10179/12954

'Split Family Expatriation: Perspectives from expatriates and their career spouses', Yvonne McNulty and Kate Hutchings, *Research Handbook of Global Families: Implications for International Business*, Edward Elgar, 2018

'What Motivates Successful Marathon Runners? The Role of Sex, Age, Education, and Training Experience in Polish Runners', Waskiewicz et al., *Front. Psychol.*, July 2019: https://www.frontiersin.org/articles/10.3389/fpsyg.2019.01671/full

'Expatriate Family Narratives on International Mobility: Key Characteristics of the Successful Moveable Family', Mila Lazarova, Yvonne McNulty and Monica Semeniuk, Liisa Mäkelä and Vesa Suutari (Eds.), *Work and Family Interface in the International Career Context*, Springer, 2015

'When long-distance relationships become geographically close', Laura Stafford, Andy Merolla, Janessa Castle, *Journal of Social and Personal Relationships*, 2006

Articles

'Lost in the Move Abroad', Robin Pascoe, *The Telegraph*, September 2014:
https://www.telegraph.co.uk/expat/4193662/Lost-in-the-move-abroad.html

'Why Resentment Lasts – and How to Defeat It', Robert Enright, *Psychology Today*, March 2017:
https://www.psychologytoday.com/us/blog/the-forgiving-life/201703/why-resentment-lasts-and-how-defeat-it

'The Curse of Emotional Needs', Steven Stosny, *Psychology Today*, July 2019:
https://www.psychologytoday.com/us/blog/anger-in-the-age-entitlement/201907/the-curse-emotional-needs

Bibliography

'Being assertive: Reduce stress, communicate better', *MayoClinic.org*, May 2020:
https://www.mayoclinic.org/healthy-lifestyle/stress-management/in-depth/assertive/art-20044644

'The Power of Small Wins', Teresa M Amabile and Steven J Kramer, *Harvard Business Review*, May 2011:
https://hbr.org/2011/05/the-power-of-small-wins?fbcl

'Why You Should Invest In Yourself', Amy Modglin, *Forbes*, January 2020: https://www.forbes.com/sites/forbescoachescouncil/2020/01/08/why-you-should-invest-in-yourself/#3333bec7017d

'Research: The Biggest Culture Gaps Are Within Countries, Not Between Them', Bradley Kirkman, Vas Taras and Piers Steel, *Harvard Business Review*, May 2016:
https://hbr.org/2016/05/research-the-biggest-culture-gaps-are-within-countries-not-between-them)

'How to Spot Each Myers-Briggs® Personality Type in Conversation', Susan Storm, *Psychology Junkie*, June 2018:
https://www.psychologyjunkie.com/2018/06/19/how-to-spot-each-myers-briggs-personality-type-in-conversation

'Please, Don't Call Me a Trailing Spouse', Claire Bolden McGill, *Global Living Magazine*, Issue 17, March/April 2015:
http://www.globallivingmagazine.com/dont-call-me-a-trailing-spouse

'The Challenges and Opportunities in Managing a Health Condition Abroad', Carolyn Parse Rizzo, *Families in Global Transition*, March 2019:
https://www.figt.org/blog/7215006

'16 Strategies to manage a health condition abroad', Vivian Chiona, April 2018:
https://www.expatnest.com/managing-a-health-condition-abroad-16-strategies-to-support-you

'Being Married to Someone with a Dangerous Job', Julia Austin, *Madame Noire*, September 2018:
https://madamenoire.com/1039402/being-married-to-someone-with-a-dangerous-job/15

'Can You Really Parent Long Distance?', *National Public Radio*, 2014:
https://www.npr.org/2014/01/21/264526795/can-you-really-parent-long-distance

'Divorce & Long Distance Parenting: How to Cope With Being Away', Chris Illuminati, *Fatherly*, June 2018:
https://www.fatherly.com/love-money/divorce-long-distance-parenting-cope-with-being-away/

'Long-Distance Fathering: Making the Most of a Difficult Situation', Ken Canfield, Charisma Magazine, 2012:
https://www.charismamag.com/life/men/16962-long-distance-fathering-making-the-most-of-a-difficult-situation

Bibliography

'5 simple tips to help you have a real conversation with a teen', Shelja Sen, *Ideas.TED.com*, Jan 2018: https://ideas.ted.com/5-simple-tips-to-help-you-have-a-real-conversation-with-a-teen/

'How to run a marathon – free marathon training plans for every kind of runner', Jane McGuire, *Runner's World*, January 2019: https://www.runnersworld.com/uk/training/marathon/a776459/marathon-training-plans/

'Orphan Spouse: How to Best Cope with Ambiguous Loss?', interview with Pauline Boss, *Expatriate Connection*, September 2013: http://expatriateconnection.com/orphan-spouse-how-to-best-cope-with-ambiguous-loss/

'Four Habits of Discipline my SEAL Dad Taught Me', Sean Kernan, *Medium*, May 2020: https://medium.com/mind-cafe/four-habits-of-discipline-my-seal-dad-taught-me-7ed9b13987df

'How to run a marathon (and enjoy it)', DD Guttenplan, *The Guardian*, August 2008

'How Bad Do You Want It: Motivation vs. Commitment', Carrie Cheadle, March 2017: https://www.carriecheadle.com/how-bad-do-you-want-it-motivation-vs-commitment/

Quotes

"Maybe it's a good idea to write something about you in my book. At least then, there will be a place where we will meet every day and be together forever!" Anamika Mishra in Caleb, 'Anamika Mishra: From Engineering to Becoming a Novelist Sensation', *Lifehacks*:
www.lifehacks.io/anamika-mishra

"Each of us has that right, that possibility, to invent ourselves daily. If a person doesn't invent herself, she will be invented. So, to be bodacious enough to invent ourselves is wise." Maya Angelou: Maya Angelou Facebook Page, March 2019:
https://www.facebook.com/MayaAngelou/photos/a.485196574795/10157930166839796/?type=3

"Due to the hours they work and the stress they're under you will be alone a lot. My husband was constantly travelling, leaving me alone in Singapore for weeks on end. I got lonely and missed my relationship with him." Character 32, '8 Reasons Why Expat Living Causes Stress and Strains on Your Relationships', May 2018:
http://www.character32.com/c32-stress-management-blog/2018/5/8/8-reasons-why-expat-living-causes-stress-and-strains-your-relationships

"Assertiveness allows for the confident expression of your needs and feelings without the need for proof. Being assertive means expressing your wants while being mindful of the opinions, feelings and wants of others." Judy Murphy, *Assertiveness, How to Stand Up for Yourself and Still Earn the Respect of Others*, CreateSpace, 2011

Bibliography

"The process of identifying your *NEEDS!* involves peeling away the layers of the onion of the unhappiness and dissatisfaction in your life." Dr Jim Taylor, 'Personal Growth: Identify Your Needs and NEEDS', *Psychology Today*, April 2012:
https://www.psychologytoday.com/us/blog/the-power-prime/201204/personal-growth-identify-your-needs-and-needs

"Even though you're growing up, you should never stop having fun." Nina Dobrev:
https://www.azquotes.com/quote/79654

"Self-awareness is the ability to see ourselves clearly, to understand who we are, how others see us, and how we fit into the world. Self-awareness gives us power." Dr Tasha Eurich, 'Increase your self-awareness with one simple fix,' TEDxMileHigh:
https://www.youtube.com/watch?v=tGdsOXZpyWE

"Be patient with yourself. Self-growth is tender; it's holy ground. There's no greater investment." Dr Stephen R Covey, *The 7 Habits of Highly Effective People*, Simon and Schuster, 2020

"Growth doesn't just happen." John C Maxwell, *The 15 Invaluable Laws of Growth: Live Them and Reach Your Potential*, Center Street, 2014

"I find it fascinating that most people plan their vacations with better care than they plan their lives. Perhaps that is because escape is easier than change." Jim Rohn, Jim Rohn Facebook Page, 29 January 2018: https://www.facebook.com/OfficialJimRohn/posts/10159891756625635

"Believing and investing in yourself is the best way to shift your thinking from a paradigm of excuses to one of solutions." Farshad Asl, The *'No Excuses' Mindset: A Life of Purpose, Passion and Clarity*, Author Academy Elite, 2016

"Baby steps are the royal road to skill." Daniel Coyle, *The Talent Code: Greatness isn't born, it's grown*, Arrow, 2010

"I exist in two places, here and where you are." Margaret Atwood, *Selected Poems: 1965-1975*, Houghton Mifflin Harcourt, 1987

"Never go to bed mad. Stay up and fight." Phyllis Diller, *Phyllis Diller's Housekeeping Hints*, Fawcett Crest Books, 1968

"In an ideal marriage, we do not merge but maintain our separateness and differing ideas." Phyllis Adler, 'Foreword' in *A Moveable Marriage: Relocate Your Relationship Without Breaking It*, Robin Pascoe, Expatriate Press Limited, 2003

"If we are going to live with our deepest differences then we must learn about one another." Deborah J Levine, *The Matrix Model Management System: Guide to Cross-Cultural Wisdom*, Deborah Levine Enterprises, 2013

Bibliography

"When dealing with life's problems, we tend to go back to our roots, which gives us a sense of comfort and identity. But the ways we choose may be perplexing to our partners." Dugan Romano, *Intercultural Marriage: Promises & Pitfalls*, Intercultural Press, 2008

"A story to me means a plot where there is some surprise. Because that is how life is – full of surprises." Isaac Bashevis Singer, *The New York Times*, 26 November 1978

"To care for those who once cared for us is one of the highest honors." Tia Walker, *The Inspired Caregiver: Finding Joy While Caring for Those You Love*, CreateSpace Independent Publishing Platform, 2013

"As a parent, you are more important than you know." Kathlene Seney-Williams, *Surviving and Thriving on the Single-Parent Journey: A Step-By-Step Approach*, Lion Books, 2019

"My best advice, whether you've been a long-distance parent for a week or ten years, is *do something*! Your child will be glad and so will you." George Newman, *101 Ways to be a Long-Distance Super-Dad or Mum, Too!*, Blossom Valley Press, 2006

"Affirming words from moms and dads are like light switches. Speak a word of affirmation at the right moment in a child's life and it's like lighting up a whole roomful of possibilities." Gary Smalley, *Leaving the Light On: Build the Memories That Will Draw Your Kids Home*, Multnomah Books, 1991

"Before I got married, I had six theories about bringing up children. Now, I have six children and no theories." Anonymous:
https://quoteinvestigator.com/2015/04/26/

"I would keep his toothbrush and toothpaste that lived in our Swiss apartment. He also had half the closet space. So, when he got there, he had his stuff. It wasn't like a stranger coming into the apartment, it was like 'you fit here'." Interview of Sundae Schneider-Bean, 'Solo Parenting Expat Mums', 22 May 2020

"I think moms, single or not, put a lot of pressure on ourselves trying to balance it all. It's NEVER going to be perfectly balanced – the sooner you know this, the sooner you can relieve some of the pressure you put on yourself." Denise Richards in 'Interview with Denise Richards: Career, Motherhood, Body Image, Charlie Sheen and More...', Erica Diamond:
https://ericadiamond.com/interview-with-denise-richards-career-motherhood-body-image-charlie-sheen-and-more/

"If you want to run, run a mile. If you want to experience a different life, run a marathon." Emil Zátopek in 'Zátopek was known as the 'Czech Locomotive' because of his conspicuous wheezing and groaning', Michael Shermer, June 2016:
https://michaelshermer.com/articles/emil-zatopek-greatest-runner-youve-never-heard-of/

Bibliography

"Key stakeholders can make or break the success of a project. Even if all the deliverables are met and the objectives are satisfied, if your key stakeholders aren't happy, nobody's happy." Adrienne Watt, *Project Management*, BCcampus Open Education: https://opentextbc.ca/projectmanagement/

"Showing up begins long before you stand at the start." Gina Greenlee, *The Whole Person Guide to Your First Marathon: A Mind, Body, Spirit Companion*, 2013

"No marriage, or life, is static, however much we might wish that things would stay the same. People change. Some marriages can't handle transformations and growth." Phyllis Adler, 'Foreword' in Robin Pascoe, *A Moveable Marriage: Relocate Your Relationship Without Breaking It*, Expatriate Press Limited, 2003

"What we may not realise is that, in many cases, the failure of a marriage stems not from an impossible situation but from the couple's inability to work things through." Phyllis Adler, 'Foreword' in Robin Pascoe, *A Moveable Marriage: Relocate Your Relationship Without Breaking It*, Expatriate Press Limited, 2003

"Listen to your body, it could be that something is being depleted. Ask yourself how you can refuel." Interview of Sundae Schneider-Bean, 'Solo Parenting Expat Mums', 22 May 2020

"Each day brings new life, new strength, new dreams and new hope. May you find courage, confidence and hope to reach out for your dreams." Lailah Gifty Akita

"No matter how well you plan, your project can always encounter unexpected problems." Adrienne Watt, *Project Management*, BCcampus Open Education:
https://opentextbc.ca/projectmanagement/

"Your body provides you with constant feedback that can help improve your running performance while minimizing biomechanical stress. Learn to differentiate between the discomfort of effort and the pain of injury. When you practice listening, you increase competence in persevering through the former and responding with respect and compassion to the latter." Gina Greenlee, *The Whole Person Guide to Your First Marathon: A Mind, Body, Spirit Companion*, 2013

"It's as if we're in a harness, we work alongside each other, just 300 miles apart." Debbie Horsfield (writer), *Poldark*, Season 4, Episode 6, 2018

"Where the marathon starts is after 30 kilometers. That's where you feel pain everywhere in your body. The muscles are really aching, and only the most prepared and well-organized athlete is going to do well after that." Eliud Kipchoge, 'Secrets of success from Eliud Kipchoge, the greatest marathon runner ever', October 2020:
https://value.co.ke/article/31-eliud-kipchoge-quotes-inspiring-quotes-eliud-kipchoge

Other Sources

'Stress', *Cleveland Clinic*:
https://my.clevelandclinic.org/health/articles/11874-stress

'Cultural Values: Definition, Examples and Importance', Juli Yelnick: www.study.com

Be Vocal: Speak Up for Mental Health:
https://www.bevocalspeakup.com/how-to-be-vocal-for-yourself.html

Podcast Episodes

'Dual career couples & putting the business at the same level as the partner's job', *Tandem Nomads' Podcast*, Episode 168, May 2020

'Long-Distance Survival Guide with Christine Gerber Rutt', *Expat Happy Hour*, Episode 161

Surveys

'The Holding the Fort Abroad Survey', *A Multicultural Life*:
www.amulticulturallife.com/holding-the-fort

'The Way We Work in 2025 and Beyond', *PricewaterhouseCoopers*:
https://www.pwc.ch/en/publications/2017/the-way-we-work-hr-today_pwc-en_2017.pdf

'Expat Insider 2018', *InterNations*:
https://cms-internationsgmbh.netdna-ssl.com/cdn/file/
cms-media/public/2018-09/Expat-Insider-2018_The-
InterNations-Survey.pdf

The Self-Nurture Survey, part of The Thymes Limited's
Take Thymes for Yourself public awareness campaign, in
partnership with Dr Alice Domar:
https://www.ipsos.com/en-us/80-women-recognize-
value-self-nurture-yet-few-care-selves-they-care-others

Videos

'Interview with Dr Stuart Brown', University of Minnesota
Bakken Centre for Spirituality and Healing:
https://youtu.be/C9mEyuZ6Ir8

'We Lived Two Parallel Lives', Military Kids Connect:
https://militarykidsconnect.health.mil/Military-Life/
Family

Appendix 1:
Couples Split by Covid-19

Blogpost 'When will I see you again?' on www. amulticulturallife.com in July 2020.

If he doesn't show, I have no way of getting in contact with him, I realise, as the boys and I drive to the airport to pick up my husband. It is the 6th of March 2020 and he is due back for three weeks from his overseas posting. With all the borders closing due to the coronavirus pandemic, there is a very real chance he could get stuck on his way home.

A year ago, we made the decision to live in separate countries. We always said we would never do it, but circumstances aligned, and it seemed like the best decision for the whole family. Our ageing parents needed at least one of us closer by, our eldest was in a pivotal school year, the job offered in Kabul was my husband's dream job. We agreed with each other that he would come back for every school holiday, and I felt I could handle the school terms... But we hadn't factored in a pandemic.

The boys and I wait nervously as passengers walk through Arrivals. The only option would be for us to drive an hour and a half back home and check for any messages from him there. Making contingency plans has become a habit, as it goes hand in hand with the international, global life.

Finally, after what seems like an endless wait, there he is. We have not seen him for 10 weeks. The relief I feel at the sight of him is indescribable. We hug and kiss and drag him to the car. On the way home everyone talks at the same time, eager to update him on family news. The conversation then shifts to the coronavirus and what it means for our country, our relatives, and our friends. We have extended family in four countries and friends on every continent. At the end of March, I was due to speak in Bangkok at the Annual Conference of Families in Global Transition on the topic of living as an expat with a travelling partner, but it quickly got cancelled. We have been following the virus on the news as it has wormed its way around the world.

After a few days, the Swiss government put in place social distancing. For us this is good news, as this must surely mean we will live lockdown together. "I am so sorry, my darling," my husband says, however, as he hugs me tight. "I feel so torn. As the leader of the team, I need to go back and take decisions in these difficult times, but I also want to stay with you." It is gut-wrenching, but I understand; these are not easy times and I know that if he could, he would stay with us.

My main concern is being the only adult in the house. What if I get sick? Who will take care of the children?

Appendix 1

And if he gets sick, how will he be evacuated back if there are no flights? Without knowing about the decision that had just been made, close friends call offering to be our back-up adults if needed. I feel a weight off my shoulders. As to whether we can see each other if one of us gets sick is an uncertainty we are going to have to live with, as is not knowing when we will see each other again.

So we find ourselves, on the 19th of March 2020, on our way to the airport again, to drop Papa back off. My stomach is in knots, I am having difficulty swallowing.

The airport is eerily quiet; I do not think we have ever seen one so empty. A handful of flights light up one third of a screen, otherwise completely black, including the two screens beside it. A few people hurry by, heads down, frantically trying to avoid too close a contact with other passengers on their way to Departures. We hug and wave goodbye as Papa walks away. I am grateful we have been able to see him for two weeks.

The last year has been spent researching and interviewing for *Holding the Fort Abroad*, my book on expat families where one of the partners travels a lot for work, so I know that there are more families in similar situations (to be published in March 2021 by Summertime Publishing).

A few days later, the private Facebook group 'Solo Parenting Expat Mums' is born. Stories start coming in: an American mum in Kenya, her husband stuck in

Sudan, his planned R&R (rest & recuperation) cancelled a few days before he was due to fly home, a husband who stays in China while his wife and kids travel back to the UK, a French mum visiting her adult children, unable to return to be with her husband in Iran, to name just a few. These were not planned separate living arrangements! These were sudden, emotionally violent, tearing-apart of families. On top of managing the challenges of living across cultures and countries, families are now dealing with taking decisions about geographically separating, reuniting after times apart and parenting together across the miles. The parent with the children worries about being the only adult in the home and sees no reprieve from day-to-day parenting. The posts in the group revolve around these themes and coaching guides are available to help members find workable solutions for their circumstances.

Appendix 2:
Life Satisfaction & Life Balance

This is an exercise we do in Coaching. It enables you to take a snapshot, at a given time, of where you are at in different areas of your life. It is essential to review it regularly, especially as you work on the different areas.

On a scale of 1 to 10 (1 being the least satisfied and 10 being the most satisfying), how would you rate each area of your life?

Areas unaffected by partner's travel

Physical health   _____

Working on your own
projects/passions/personal development plans _____

Relationships with extended family   _____

Personal spiritual life/well-being   _____

Taking care of my needs   _____

Financial stability   _____

Physical environment (Home, Cars,
Neighbourhood, etc.)   _____

If you think that one of the above is affected by your partner's travels, then move it to the columns on the next page and rate it there.

When your partner is not travelling

Relationship with your partner   _____
Relationships with kids   _____
Home management   _____
Friends/Social life/Hobbies   _____
Feeling safe   _____

When your partner is travelling

Relationship with your partner   _____
Relationships with kids   _____
Home management   _____
Friends/Social life/Hobbies   _____
Feeling safe   _____

You may have rated 'Physical Health' as a 4, for example. Now ask yourself the following question: what one action can I take to make the rate I give it go up to a 5?

Look at the areas you have given a high mark to. What are you doing in those areas that you can transfer to other areas of your life?

Choose one area to work on. You can't do it all at once.

Appendix 3:
Personal Development Plan

You may already know what you want to work towards in terms of acquiring new skills for a hobby, a passion or a career. If you don't, start planting S.E.E.D.S (see *Keep Growing* in *Chapter 2*), then come back and do this plan.

Your PDP doesn't need to be complicated. In fact, this is going to be a very simple framework. If you want to go into more detail, I recommend you visit the UK's Open University Page: https://help.open.ac.uk/pdp

Okay, let's get started, shall we?

Step 1: Achievements

1.1   List your educational achievements:

_____

_____

_____

_____

_____

_____

_____

1.2   List your professional skills:

_____

_____

_____

_____

_____

1.3   List your personal skills/achievements, e.g. cooking, moving ☺ :

_____   _____

_____   _____

_____   _____

_____   _____

1.4   Ask five people who know you well to write down your strengths and skills. Ask them for examples of when and how they saw that strength/skill displayed. Collate the examples.

_____

_____

_____

_____

_____

_____

_____

_____

Step 2: Vision

2.1.   Describe an ideal day, either at work (if you are looking to develop a career) or in your private life.

_____

_____

_____

_____

_____

_____

_____

_____

_____

_____

_____

Step 3: New Skills

3.1.   Where do you need more PRACTICE?

_____

_____

_____

_____

3.2.   Where do you need more TRAINING? (Set dates and times when you will do research.)

_____

_____

_____

_____

_____

_____

3.3.   Where do you need MENTORS?

_____

_____

_____

_____

_____

_____

Step 4: Set a date to review this PDP.

4.1.   What have you been able to do?

_____

_____

_____

_____

_____

4.2.   What still needs to be done?

_____

_____

_____

_____

_____

_____

_____

_____

_____

4.3.   What needs to change?

_____

_____

_____

_____

_____

_____

_____

_____

_____

_____

_____

_____

_____

_____

_____

Appendix 4:
Checklists – Preparing for Time Apart

My Couple

1. How and when will we spend time together before starting this 'Marathon'?

    ☐ _____

    ☐ _____

    ☐ _____

    ☐ _____

    ☐ _____

2. How do we each feel 'held in mind' by the other person? (Take turns answering and taking notes.)

    I feel 'held in mind' when:

    ☐ _____

    ☐ _____

    ☐ _____

    ☐ _____

    ☐ _____

My partner feels 'held in mind' when:

☐ _____

☐ _____

☐ _____

☐ _____

☐ _____

3. How do we share life while we are apart? How do we stay connected?

_____

_____

_____

_____

_____

_____

4. How often will we communicate? (Be explicit. Will you make a point of saying 'good morning' and 'goodnight' to each other, even if that is the only exchange you have on certain days? You may need to be flexible with this and adjust to time available once the 'Marathon' starts.)

☐ Secure App, Marco Polo
☐ Impromptu pictures and texts
☐ Weekly Update Email
☐ Logistics conversations
☐ Couple phone date

5. Would we like to exchange a personal item that the other can treasure while apart?

☐ Yes
☐ No

My Children

1. Would you like to lend Daddy/Mummy a stuffed toy or something precious as a treasure from home?

☐ Yes
☐ No

2. Read a book or play a game about expressing feelings. (See *Resources* for a list of books.)

3. Ask the children how they are going to communicate to me when they are worried.

My Support Network

1. Who is offering what? Be specific. If a friend is offering you 'help' they will say something general like, "Give me a shout if you need anything." Make sure to have a discussion with them about *what* they could offer. This includes outings, meals, childcare, call in case of emergency, prayer.

_____

_____

_____

_____

_____

_____

_____

_____

_____

2. Who will regularly check up on me?

_____

_____

_____

_____

_____

3. Who will support me emotionally?

_____

_____

_____

_____

_____

_____

_____

About the Author

Founder of A Multicultural Life and a Certified Life Coach, Rhoda helps expat mums with a travelling partner reduce overload, work on their personal projects, parent and thrive as a couple and have smoother reconnections when the travelling partner comes home from a business trip.

Born to a Welsh father and a Syrian-Armenian mother, raised as a Missionary Kid in France, now married to a Swiss, Rhoda realised just how multicultural she was a few years ago, when she hired a Life Coach. She and her family had moved from NYC to Switzerland and she just didn't want to start from scratch again. She had moved as an adult about 10 times in 20 years, as a single person to begin with, then as a married person. She had lost her sense of self on the way and didn't know what she wanted to do. The children were a bit older and she wanted to build something for herself that would work with their life. The coaching changed her life and her outlook so much that she trained as a Life Coach. She also looked into multicultural dynamics, especially applying to families, and many hidden sources of conflict were resolved.

As she and her husband started talking about him working away from home for longer periods of time, that's when it hit her: he had basically been travelling the whole of their marriage. When reading about the stresses for Accompanying Partners, their partner's long hours at work and travelling is always mentioned in bulk along with being in a new place, loss of social network, loss of job, and so on. Around the same time, a friend of hers, who is from the US, mentioned her husband's travel felt different to when he was travelling 'back home'. This piqued Rhoda's interest as she had only known being an expat wife with a travelling husband.

Since then, she has been focusing on the travelling part of expat life, which has culminated in this book.

For personal coaching or to share your story, contact Rhoda on:

Website: www.amulticulturallife.com

LinkedIn: www.linkedin.com/in/rhodabangerteramulticulturallife

Facebook page: www.facebook.com/amulticulturallife

Facebook group: 'Solo Parenting Expat Mums'

Instagram: www.instagram.com/amulticulturallife

Also by Summertime Publishing
and Springtime Books

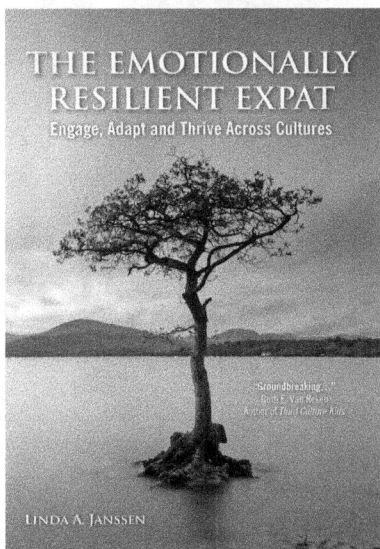

FOREWORD BY DOUG OTA

EMOTIONAL
RESILIENCE
AND THE EXPAT CHILD

Practical tips and storytelling techniques
that will strengthen the global family

Julia Simens

THE EMOTIONALLY
RESILIENT EXPAT
Engage, Adapt and Thrive Across Cultures

"Groundbreaking..."
Ruth E. Van Reken
Author of Third Culture Kids

LINDA A. JANSSEN

RAISING
GLOBAL TEENS

A Practical Handbook For
Parenting in the 21st Century

Dr. Anisha Abraham

"AN OUTSTANDING NEW ADDITION
TO THE GLOBAL FAMILY LITERATURE"

THIS
MESSY
MOBILE
LIFE

HOW A MOLA CAN HELP
GLOBALLY MOBILE FAMILIES
CREATE A LIFE BY DESIGN

MARIAM NAVAID OTTIMOFIORE

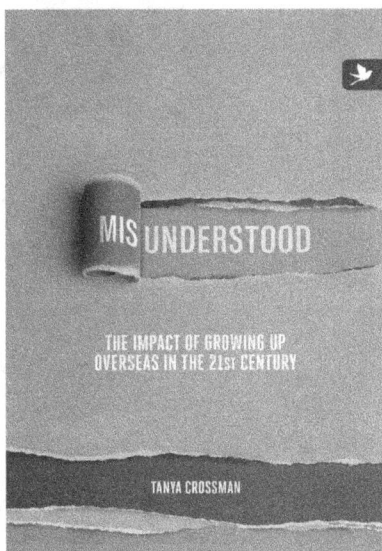

MIS UNDERSTOOD

THE IMPACT OF GROWING UP
OVERSEAS IN THE 21st CENTURY

TANYA CROSSMAN

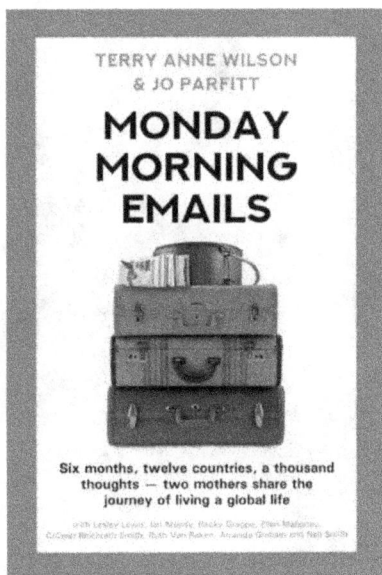

TERRY ANNE WILSON
& JO PARFITT

MONDAY
MORNING
EMAILS

Six months, twelve countries, a thousand
thoughts — two mothers share the
journey of living a global life

with Lesley Lewis, Jan Ntambi, Becky Grappo, Ellen Mahoney,
O'Cean Brichoeto Smith, Ruth Van Reken, Amanda Graham and Nell Smith

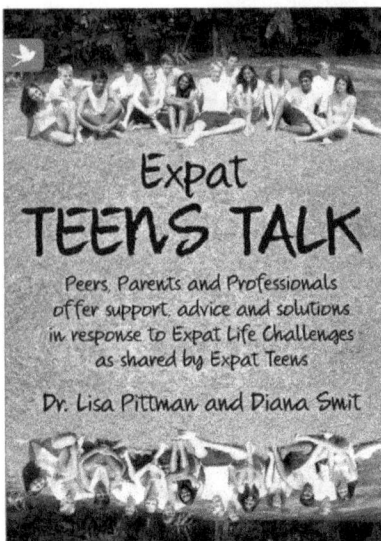

Expat
TEENS TALK

Peers, Parents and Professionals
offer support, advice and solutions
in response to Expat Life Challenges
as shared by Expat Teens

Dr. Lisa Pittman and Diana Smit

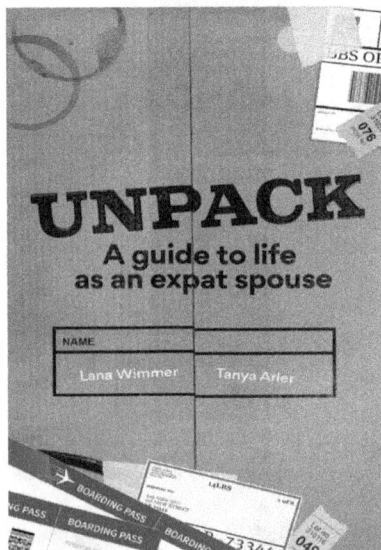

UNPACK
A guide to life
as an expat spouse

NAME

Lana Wimmer   Tanya Arler

www.ingramcontent.com/pod-product-compliance
Lightning Source LLC
Chambersburg PA
CBHW062050270326
41931CB00013B/3018